g **Misery**

ₐ anthology of essays by
women in humanitarian responses

Chasing Misery: An anthology of essays by women in humanitarian responses
Published 2014
www.chasingmisery.com

ISBN: 978-1495961465

Cover Photo: Rwandans gather at the Songore Transit Camp in Ngozi Province, Northern
Burundi. In 2006, over 4,500 people were seeking political asylum in Burundi but found the
conditions at the Songore Transit Camp to be poor. Four year old shelters, only 30 working
latrines and inadequate water supply, left many people sleeping outside in deplorable conditions. After a number of months, the Rwandan and Burundian governments struck a deal
that allowed the Rwandan army to enter the transit camp and forcibly repatriate people back
across the border. ©Jenn Warren

To all the women in our lives.

Those who raised, taught, befriended, challenged, encouraged and inspired us; to our colleagues and mentors; to those we have helped and those who have helped us.

Even if you are no longer with us; even if you are alone and far from home; even if you have been forced to flee and buried children and friends as you did so; even if you have scars that will never go away.

In our lifetimes, we have watched you hold up half the sky and what you read here is who we were brave enough to become because of you.

"Unblinking, Chasing Misery shows the humanity in humanitarian work, through the eyes of women on the front lines - from Katrina to South Sudan and beyond. These beautifully written, personal, honest and raw essays provide the reader with a rare glimpse into that world of humanitarian aid. Far from what you hear on the nightly news, the diverse stories in Chasing Misery are at their core about individuals, often rejecting stereotypes of what a woman in aid work "should" be like.

What motivates any of us to do the work we do? And more importantly, does that work make a difference? For whom? Like the women authors in the book, I was pulled by a gravitational force to "help". I founded FilmAid International in response to the refugee crisis in Kosovo and have since worked with communities in crisis in Afghanistan, Kenya, Haiti and more. The gritty, funny and inspiring stories in this book will relate to us all. Not only those who have "been in the field."

A must read!!!!"

- Caroline Baron, Founder of FilmAid International (filmaid.org)

Table Of Contents

Preface

I feel incredibly lucky to be holding this book in my hands. Not only because it is the culmination of a long-held personal desire to compile and share the stories of amazing women in humanitarian aid work but also because of the substance of the volume—the empathy, solidarity and vulnerability that the contributors have chosen to convey.

When we initially put out the call for essay and photograph submissions we had few requirements. We asked that essays, or photographs had been written, or taken, by a woman who worked in any humanitarian response in the past 10 years. As the essays came in, it was clear that the past decade has not been kind to our world—war, poverty, and natural disasters continue to overwhelm the capacity of humankind to respond to them. While many of us tend to have preconceived notions about where disasters will strike and where humanitarian aid is necessary these essays show that disasters—and accompanying misery—are indiscriminate. When the capacity of a community, or country, to respond to that disaster is overwhelmed, humanitarian aid becomes necessary. And, as necessary in America and Japan as in Syria and parts of Africa.

There is a lot of debate at the moment around humanitarian aid and a great many books, journals, and newspaper articles have been published debating its efficacy. This book is not intended to contribute to the debate. Rather, it is an attempt to describe, through the eyes of women who do the work, what it is, or was, like. There's a quote by Susan Minot which says, "People look at authors and think they're trying to tell their story. But really what they're trying to say is what it's like to be alive." This book isn't intended to make aid work look glamorous or to suggest that aid workers are "great people doing great things." It's not meant to argue for, or against, humanitarian aid. Instead, through the essays and photographs, contributors are saying, "Look, here's a sliver of human existence full of suffering and misery, and also joy, and laughter, and amazing people. This is what it's like to be alive."

A number of people have asked why the writing and photography in this book was limited to women. Obviously, men have also contributed much to aid efforts in the past decade. However, I believe that women's voices, perspectives and narratives on aid work are unique and deserve their own space. I was astounded that nearly every essay submission we received revealed a huge capacity for honesty, self-reflection and vulnerability. I strongly believe that women have a special insight and ability to explore the greys, the 'inbetweenness', to reflect on the questions about being human that plague us in our quiet moments. I believe that women are more apt to cry, or, at least, admit to crying—which, in the face of human misery and suffering, is often the only appropriate response.

Some people might feel that our telling stories from the perspective of aid workers detracts from the stories of those we have gone to help or those who are 'truly' suffering. It is a valid perspective but one with which I respectfully disagree. Humanitarianism and aid work at its core is about solidarity. It is about saying, "you are human, as I am human, and if you must suffer abject and miserable circumstances the least that I can do is be there with you, attempt to alleviate it in some way and let you know that you are not alone, that your suffering—whether from a cyclone, a war, a tsunami, or poverty—is not forgotten. It is seen and it matters. You matter. And I will tell your story through my story." That is what this anthology of essays is really about.

Humanitarian aid work is difficult and it takes its toll on the people who do it. It is stressful. It requires intense, long hours in insecure environments, observing desperate and miserable situations. In addition, aid workers often feel guilty about sharing their experiences, or seeking help, because they know that those they were helping were (and sometimes remain) in far worse conditions. At times, aid workers can suffer from guilt of not being able to help enough or being able to leave those situations. Some aid workers return from an emergency with the Post Traumatic Stress Disorder (PTSD) associated with having been in traumatic circumstances.

Caregivers, or emergency responders, in some countries are required by professional codes, or law, to have psycho-social support provided to them. Counsellors have to have a certain number of hours of counselling themselves; police officers and medics can seek counselling and resources to help them deal with difficult situations they have encountered. In the same way, humanitarian aid workers need the same sort of support because of what they've seen and engaged with. To this end we're working with the non-profit, Headington Institute (www.headington-institute.org) to support women in aid work to get the help they need and to remove any stigma or guilt attached to seeking that help. The Headington

Institute has, and continues, to develop resources to help women in aid work. Please visit their website to find out more.

As we were compiling this collection there was vigorous debate about how to order the essays and photographs. Should it be by theme? By country? How do we introduce all the different essays so that they are understandable to someone who has never heard of humanitarian aid and doesn't know where Congo is, as well as to veteran humanitarian aid workers? We finally decided on separating the book into different parts—each of which has an introduction with a few background details about the country or disaster which brought the essayist there in the first place. You will also find pictures peppered throughout the book. Where possible these link directly to the country or disaster the essays are about but, in others, we felt that the pictures were powerful enough that they could stand alone even if the country in which they were taken is not written about. The book, thus, can either be read straight through or can be dipped in and out of depending on your interest.

Lastly, I am incredibly grateful to a large number of people who have sacrificed to make this compilation a reality. Special thanks is due to the editorial team who volunteered countless hours to editing and reviewing the volume. Thanks is also due to each of the collaborators who went above and beyond simply writing and submitting their pieces but have helped in reviewing, publicising and sharing the work. I'd also like to personally thank my friends, family and supporters who not only championed the idea but also contributed funding to make it happen.

I am incredibly proud of each essay and photograph that is in here and the women who chose to share them. It takes courage to do aid work but it takes bravery to put your thoughts and experiences out in front of the world. I hope that this book both inspires and challenges you as it has me.

Kelsey Hoppe
Head of the Editorial Team
28 February 2014

Chasing Misery can be found online at: www.chasingmisery.com and on Facebook at: www.facebook.com/chasingmisery1.

Acronyms

Every profession has its own language, phraseology and vocabulary. Humanitarian aid is no different. There are a huge number of acronyms and phrases that are used routinely. For ease of reading and understanding, in some cases you will find acronyms spelled out at their first usage and, for others that are very common, you won't. Below are a number of acronyms you will find while reading.

AIDS   a disease in which there is a severe loss of the body's cellular immunity, greatly lowering the resistance to infection and malignancy

AK-47 a type of assault rifle, originally manufactured in the former Soviet Union

BBC   the British Broadcasting Corporation

CAR   Central African Republic

CPA   Comprehensive Peace Agreement - an agreement which ended a 20+ year civil war between Northern and Southern Sudan

DRC   Democratic Republic of Congo

EU   European Union

GPS   Global Positioning System

HIV   the Human Immunodeficiency Virus which causes AIDS

HQ   Headquarters

IDP   internally displaced person—a person who is displaced within a country rather than someone who has fled over a border who is known as a refugee

IVs   intravenous—a device that is used to allow a fluid (such as blood or a liquid medication) to flow directly into a patient's veins

KG   kilogram

LRA   Lord's Resistance Army—a rebel group that originated in Northern Uganda

M23   the 'March 23 Movement' (also known as the Congolese Revolutionary Army) is a rebel military group based in eastern areas of the Democratic Republic of the Congo

NGO   Non-Governmental Organisation

OLS   Operation Lifeline Sudan - a consortium of UN agencies and approximately 35 non-governmental organizations operating in southern Sudan during the civil war

PR   Public Relations

R'n'R   Rest and Relaxation—usually granted to aid workers in addition to vacation for working in hardship locations

SPLA   Sudan People's Liberation Army—previously the rebel group in Southern Sudan which fought against Sudan. Now, the army of the Republic of South Sudan.

UK   United Kingdom

UN   United Nations

UNDP   United Nations Development Program—the United Nations' global development network

UNHCR   The Office of the United Nations High Commisioner for Refugees—a United Nations agency mandated to protect and support refugees

UNICEF   United Nations Children's Fund—an agency of the United Nations responsible for programs to aid education and the health of children and mothers in developing countries

USD   United States Dollars

VHF   Very High Frequency—usually referring to a portable radio system that organisations use for communication

WFP   World Food Program - the food assistance branch of the United Nations

Chasing Misery

Kelsey Hoppe

I like to smoke here. The smoke wafts and curls and hangs indecisively in the humid air. Horrid clove cigarettes he calls them. This man who is not in love with me but thinks he is.

There'll be another earthquake, I say.

How do you know? he asks.

I just know, I shrug.

What else do you know? he asks.

I know that he is not in love with me. I know that this is how life is, that you can sit on a roof in the desperate tropical heat talking about earthquakes and fathers and religion and think that you are in love with someone that you are not.

Of course I do not say this. I say that I know because earthquakes are a problem here. The ground keeps moving in this volatile place where one day there's a volcano, and the next an earthquake and the next a giant wave that wipes out a couple hundred thousand people. I say that the trouble with the earth is that it keeps shifting.

That's a lie. I don't say any of that either. I say that there are just things that I know and this is one of them. I know that if an earthquake happened now we would die. Sitting three stories up on the roof of this concrete building in the damp night smoking. He lights another cigarette. We don't care. I don't care. What does it matter anyway if disasters keep coming? It doesn't matter to us. We are the sort of people who were supposed to die young and didn't.

So.

We parade through life dressed in immortality. Traipsing around in places where it is likely that we will be shot or drowned or kidnapped and beheaded by people who believe things a little too much. Trying our immortality on for size, like new clothes, seeing if it fits. It never does. Immortality never fits anyone.

The electricity has gone out again. All over the city. Leaving the rooftops lit only by the tired moon that is waning half-heartedly behind us. A mullah begins to wail the sad cry of the prayer call. He is joined by another then another until the air is full of their lonely mournful cries to Allah – the immortal, the all-powerful – who seems, tonight, to not be listening. The steep tile roof cracks ominously when we shift our weight. Like the earth cracking when its weight shifts beneath the problems of the city below, lying stifling hot and quiet. We are all sitting on a fault that is about to give way.

I'm leaving, I say.

When? he asks.

In a month, I say.

Where will you go? he asks.

Somewhere else, I say and look at the bright glow of the cigarette as the ash creeps toward my fingers.

Come to Vancouver, he says.

Why? I ask.

I'll be in Vancouver, he says.

Maybe, I say.

We both know that I will not come. We both know that he won't be in Canada. There will be another earthquake, another flood, another war, another reason to not go where we think we are going. It is a strange life, this. Chasing human misery around the planet. We are not the sort of people who go where we say we are going. We are not the sort of people who go places for other people. We are not people who need others to come and be where we are. This is what makes us so interesting. This is what makes us think we are in love with each other when we are not. We are in love with ourselves. We are in love with the idea of ourselves. It is actually a mad grasping fit of jealousy that we mistake as love when we see our lives being lived by another.

What time is it? I ask.

He looks at his watch. Don't know, he says.

I bet it's two in the morning, I say.

It's probably two in the morning somewhere, he says.

You use too many adverbs, I say.

Definitely, he says.

An electric storm plays on the far horizon chased by rain brushing the slums, drenching the people with concerns we don't have. Will there be food tomorrow? Will there be enough water? Our problems consist mainly of finding the money to fix these problems of which there is never enough. Money, that is. There are always enough problems.

He takes a long drag on his cigarette and flicks the stub across the roof where it rolls, trailing sparks, down the incline onto the porch below.

Do roof tiles burn? I ask.

Probably, he says.

The mullahs keep up their prayers until finally they begin to go out, one by one, like exhausted candles being extinguished by the darkness that presses on the ever cracking, shifting earth.

Real Women in Aid Work: Must We Be Either Angelina Jolie or Mother Theresa?

Melissa Philips

"Sorry Madam, you cannot go through because you have handcuffs in your bag."

With that statement I thought that the Kenyan security office at Nairobi's Jomo Kenyatta airport had ended my aid career before it began. The man who said this to me had no idea of the gravity of his words. He couldn't have known that I had taken three flights and been awake for twenty hours to get this far. And, he couldn't have known that this being my first time in Nairobi I'd grossly underestimated how long it would take to drive to the airport. He was also probably unaware that I was racing to get to a United Nations flight that would take me to Lokichoggio in the far north of Kenya which would be my first stop on the way to Rumbek, South Sudan. I was heading there to take up my first ever role with the UN, an organisation I had dreamed of working for ever since I graduated from university. I was set to take my experience with refugees and asylum-seekers to new levels, in the field of protection for displaced people. But right now I felt like I would never see that dream realised. What he had done was discover that my alarm clock looked suspiciously like handcuffs through his x-ray machine.

Faced with the prospect of my humanitarian career ending before it began I did what any sensible person would do—I started to cry. Not just a small sniffle mind you—bawling, tears, and on the brink of hysteria, I opened my case and trawled through my possessions to find and present the offending alarm clock. I was surrounded by other conflict-weary, khaki-wearing aid workers who were mostly men and I feared I had committed a fatal error that highlighted both my newness and my gender.

Finally permitted to leave by security, I pulled my disorderly possessions together and was saved by two female colleagues who were also headed to South Sudan and more airport savvy than I. Embarrassed and feeling like I'd shown weakness in being unable to handle this relatively minor setback these two people travelling on the same flight rescued me. "Pull yourself together," they ordered me, "and run to the boarding gate." Run I did, making it onto the plane to Lokichoggio and then South Sudan.

But this isn't a story about crying or trying to avoid crying (which I still have not learnt how to do), it is about women in the field of aid work and our ambiguous role. It is about why we choose it as a profession, what we bring to it and how we feel about it – and how others feel about us. Looking back on myself in the airport in Nairobi is like viewing myself through a distorted mirror. Is my impression of myself how others actually saw me, or is my perspective of myself inevitably altered due to the passage of time?

Outside of the aid world sphere, an aid worker is often presented in the media and popular press as saint and saviour; a neutral actor delivering help and in possession of heroic strength and super-human resilience in the midst of war and chaos. Typically refugee camps appear on our television screens when people like Angelina Jolie visit them, looking calm and serene. Characterisations of aid workers around her are usually stereotypical, best captured by the oft-quoted slogan that we are 'missionary, mad, or mercenary'. Additionally, most of these stereotypes rest on the assumption that aid workers are male, and overlook the fact that aid work attracts both men and women – much as you would find in most other jobs around the world. It is not that the people who work in these roles are special or different, only that the challenges vary. When I tell most people about living and working in South Sudan their comments are about how amazing my time must have been (which it was), how brave I was (something de-bunked by the story above), or asking if I felt safe (most of the time, very).

The women I knew in aid work demonstrated remarkable creativity in handling the daily challenges of working in remote locations. They knew what to do when our water supply ran out; they could find tailors deep in the bowels of any outdoor market who could sew dresses. Once a group of friends even managed to borrow a karaoke machine to host a hen party. Many of us volunteered over and above our day jobs through community projects, charity events or fundraising. Women are often the minority in any team or group. As part of a field mission, another colleague and I were the sole female members of a sizeable assessment team, going out to determine and report on issues in conflict-stricken areas. Our male counterparts arrived and immediately started to interview local authority figures and soldiers. My colleague and I instinctively walked over to speak to the women and girls sitting in the local school, to hear about the situation from their perspective. The resultant assessment report was all the better for our input by adding the perspective of women and girls. While men told us about problems with conflict and cattle, women often talked about food and family. I've asked questions about Lost Girls, girls who have lost contact with their family during the war and ended up in refugee camps mainly in Kenya, when everyone else seems to focus on the 'Lost Boys' of South Sudan. I've also learnt to remain silent at times when a relatively young woman speaking would be culturally inappropriate. Sadly I've also had to ask other women how they deal with sexism and harassment in aid work.

While there are debates by people like the Chief Operating Officer of Facebook Sheryl Sandberg about the roles of women in the workplace – the sacrifices they make and how they deal with them – the role of women in aid work should also be examined. We should be honest about the roles men and women play in aid work and the influence of gender; both positive and negative. As people who lobby and advocate for the rights of women and girls all over the world, perhaps we need to need to turn our attention inward to ourselves. Recognising the creative, unique and vital role of women in aid work goes beyond Mother Teresa analogies, or images of celebrities such as Angelina Jolie visiting refugees in dusty camps. Very little is known about the different approaches men and women bring to aid work, or even how many women are represented in this field as compared to men. Anecdotally, men still occupy more leadership roles than women in the not-for-profit sector more broadly, despite it traditionally being a female-dominated profession. One wonders if the same applies to the aid sector.

I'm still grateful to my colleagues in Nairobi for bundling me up and getting me onto that plane and into an aid work career. Later,

I would learn to appreciate my tears. I would learn that being a 'neutral' aid worker did not mean that I couldn't show any emotion. While, at times, tears were still embarrassing at others they were the only appropriate reaction to what I witnessed. Tears might be considered a display of weakness but I have learned that they express more than that – they can show solidarity and strength.

I hope that future generations of women in aid work don't feel that they have to apologise for their gender. Most importantly, I hope we find a way to develop more inclusive and realistic models for women doing aid work in the field—handcuffs and all. Doing this will require more honest and diverse accounts of what it means to be a female aid worker and an acknowledgement of the ways that gender can and does make a positive difference in aid work.

The Field: The Ever Receeding Vanishing Point
Helen Seeger

In the aid work sector, the prestige, admiration and recognition of a specific individual is directly proportional to how authentically grubby, sweaty, sunburnt and sleep-deprived he or she is.

If the layer of dirt and sweat has been accrued in more than one country, so much the better. A stylish haircut is more or less professional suicide—a 'real' aid worker would never have the time for such upkeep! During the humanitarian response to the massive floods in Pakistan in 2010, this hierarchy quickly became apparent in my office in the capital, Islamabad.

Key to this hierarchy and gaining ground within it is each staff member's proximity to a mythical place called 'The Field'. Frustratingly, however, every time I seem to get close to it, it turns out to be somewhere else, just down the road. Visitors from the organisation's headquarters in Geneva and Bangkok arrive brimming with excitement at reaching The Field, and I have the unenviable task of puncturing their enthusiasm, explaining that unfortunately Islamabad was not it. The Field is much, much further away.

After the initial panic of proposals and daily planes landing full of tents passes, I receive permission to go on a field trip to the sub-offices. "Aha!" I think. "Field trip = The Field. Awesome."

I have a hazy notion of what The Field is like. Judging from the briefing given by our cantankerous security officer, delivered while staring with intense disapproval at my sandals, it is at least two feet deep in water, ripe black water snakes making a deadly beeline straight for my vulnerable toes. Various sightings on the airplane down to the flood zone lead me to believe that it is a land where people only wear polyester quick-dry clothing, like Indiana Jones, with handy air flaps and sections which zip off.

In my whimsical daydreams, The Field appears as a remote village, where I'll spend all day in the sun, handing out bags of wheat, or mosquito nets, or water purification tablets to a long line of quietly grateful women and children. On days off, I plan to sit in a big circle with the whole village, and talk about needs and village priorities. Or I'll play football with a gang of charming and half-naked children. At night the inhabitants of The Field surely sleep in rustic safari tents with the sound of helicopters bringing in supplies over head, snoring gently after consuming two bottles of whiskey in the company of some friendly Russians, the infamous helicopter pilots about whom every veteran aid worker seems to have a story.

It's no wonder therefore that headquarters staff from DC, London or Paris are always a little bemused landing in Nairobi, Islamabad or Kabul. They've been looking forward to being in The Field for six months now, and can't wait to have some authentic, heart-warming and gently amusing incidents involving Beneficiaries (for this is what—somewhat optimistically you might say—we aid workers call the people we help) that they can post on Facebook.

So where is that village football match? Oh no, I tell the poor visitor on arrival, you've got it all wrong. Islamabad is not The Field. Even Hyderabad or Sukkur is not The Field. The Field is in [insert dustier place], where Aid Workers are Aid Workers. In Islamabad, a visitor from DC is to do all the same things they do in DC, just at a different desk on a different continent. There are proposals to be written and financial reports to be checked during the day and the evening will be spent at comfortable and familiar cocktail bars, Italian restaurants, and shopping malls. Disappointingly, there is a complete absence of smiling Beneficiaries.

I never find The Field in Pakistan. Undeterred, I plot my escape to 'The Real Field'. Yemen. It sounds sufficiently dusty. With my arrival scheduled in Sana'a I am certain that The Field must be there.

My heart rises at the sight of the chaos at baggage claim. Definitely this must be the entrance to The Field. I can almost hear the hissing of the water snakes. Emerging timidly from the airport, I peer expectantly into the dark. It is not clear whether the lines of people are Beneficiaries or taxi drivers hoping for a fare. Never mind, I'll find out tomorrow.

The next day I'm issued a laptop, a Nokia phone and a desk in the corner within handy reach of both the printer and the water cooler. Out the window is a view of a corrugated metal sheet. I'm earnestly and warmly welcomed, and told I'm here just in time. There is a proposal for UN funding due in three days, and no one has had the time to finalise the budget.

At a raucous house party that evening, it is evident that The Field has once again eluded my grasp. That pesky blighter! Always slipping away.

Sipping a gin and tonic, I mutter to myself that surely the Beneficiaries or even The Community Leaders do not have such a strong affection for the Black Eyed Peas which blares over the small speakers.

Some new friends at the party confirm my fears: the party scene in Yemen is much like that in Pakistan, only smaller and more incestuous. The combination of restricted movement, curfews, scarce alcohol and lack of any venue even vaguely resembling a bar leads to bizarre fraternity style parties where the main aim is to drink so as to numb your inhibitions enough to dance to Ke$ha. In your own living room. In the company of your work colleagues. Before the car comes to pick you up at 11pm. The parties are made more bizarre by their absolute consistency in format, style and attendance each time – week after week. After a while you feel like Bill Murray in Groundhog Day, only more hungover.

Most of the people I talk to at the party seem to have no interest in joining me on my quest for The Field. Most seem much more interested in finding some other place altogether different, which I have never heard of before. They talk repeatedly about 'The Family Duty Station' (a location where one is not prohibited by various security and insurance considerations from being allowed to live with one's spouse, partner and/or children) and 'The Headquarters Posting' (a cushy NGO/UN job in the upper echelons of the organisation, typically somewhere like Geneva, Paris, Rome or New York). These options certainly don't seem to offer much opportunity for congenial, personally-enriching meetings underneath banyan trees.

Spirits flagging somewhat below a cheery smile, I catch a flight to Aden the next day. The climate is promising—Aden is certainly hot and humid enough to be The Field. There are lots of people sitting on the side of the road, and I hope for an instant that these might be Beneficiaries. Alas, they are more interested in chewing huge balls of qat (a fresh leaf, the prolonged chewing of which produces a moderate amphetamine effect) than lining up for anything.

Arriving at the coordination meeting that I am to attend, a colleague mentions a project in Abyan that has just started. Distributions tomorrow! Maybe some focus group discussions! I almost jump for joy. Finally, I've found it.

My elation is met with blank confusion. Oh no, sorry, you must have misunderstood. There's no access to The Field for international staff at the moment, unlikely to be for quite some time in fact. But there's a well-equipped, air-conditioned office on the next street, and the field teams will send you their data tomorrow. If you could just make some graphs, write a little introductory blurb and include a photo or two, that would be perfect. And then later we'll all go the Chinese restaurant and have a few beers. Russian helicopter pilots? Well, in fact, there very well may be one or two of those...

Women waiting in line for voucher-based seed fairs to start in South Kivu, Democratic Republic of Congo. ©Emilie Greenhalgh

Borehole drilling programme for eradication of guinea worm in Terekeka, South Sudan. ©Rebekah Rice

United States — Hurricane Katrina
Introduction

In late August 2005, Hurricane Katrina hit the Gulf Coast of the United States wreaking unprecedented damage. As a Category 5 hurricane it battered the coasts of the states of Louisiana, Mississippi and Alabama with 175 mph winds.[1] In total, 1,836 people died, millions were left homeless and property damage was estimated to be $81 billion USD.[2] The National Oceanic and Atmospheric Administration (NOAA) classified it as the most destructive storm to have hit the United States.

New Orleans, in particular, experienced some of the heaviest damage when levees, that were meant to protect the city from flooding, collapsed and floodwaters reached 20 feet in some places.[3] Three days after the hurricane had passed, 80 percent of the city was still under floodwater.[4]

A mandatory evacuation of New Orleans was ordered. However, many people couldn't, or wouldn't, leave. Hundreds of thousands of people were displaced and sought refuge in the New Orleans Convention Centre and Superdome. Finding and identifying

1. Waple, Anne. "Hurricane Katrina"; December 2005; NOAA's National Climatic Data Center, Asheville, NC. Available from http://www.ncdc.noaa.gov/extremeevents/specialreports/Hurricane-Katrina.pdf.
2. Zimmerman, Kim Ann. "Hurricane Katrina: Facts, Damage & Aftermath"; Aug 2012; LiveScience. vailable from: http://www.livescience.com/22522-hurricane-katrina-facts.html.
3. Waple, Anne. "Hurricane Katrina"; December 2005; NOAA's National Climatic Data Center, Asheville, NC. Available from http://www.ncdc.noaa.gov/extremeevents/specialreports/Hurricane-Katrina.pdf.
4. Ibid.

victims who died in the storm took weeks.[5] On its own doorstep, the United States experienced the death, damage and displacement normally associated with natural disasters and wars in other countries.

5. O'Neill, Ann. "Identifying victims a grueling task"; CNN, 9 September 2005. Available from: http://www.cnn.com/2005/US/09/09/katrina.morgue/index.html.

Baker, Louisiana is home to thousands of displaced Katrina victims from New Orleans. Living in five FEMA sites, residents are far from job opportunities, anxious about their futures, and with few to speak on their behalf. ©Jenn Warren

A resident of Renaissance Village, the largest FEMA camp in Baker candidly talks about his struggles with finding work and being separated from his teenage daughter. ©Jenn Warren

Baker, Louisiana is home to thousands of displaced Katrina victims from New Orleans, including Wilber Ross. Living in five FEMA sites, residents are far from job opportunities, anxious about their futures, and with few to speak on their behalf. ©Jenn Warren

A damaged home in the Ninth Ward, New Orleans, Louisiana. Many residents of the Ninth Ward could not afford to repair their homes, which were left abandoned or lying in disrepair for years after Hurricane Katrina. ©Jenn Warren

From New Orleans to South Sudan: How I Healed by Moving to a War-Torn Country

Miranda Bryant

Hot, humid Mississippi State in the mournful, unyielding days following Hurricane Katrina. I've climbed the bleached plywood steps to knock on the tinny door of the travel trailer. The air is still. As I give it one more tap while scanning the ghostly emptiness of the sterile trailer park, the door creaks open. Hunching in the doorway, blinking into the sunlight, is a man so emaciated, so pale, I'm certain he is a breath away from the next world. I adjust my NGO-issued baseball cap and clipboard and explain my purpose. He allows me entry and we settle in at his austere table. I ask him the standard questions on the health and wellbeing questionnaire: What is your worst problem since coming to live in this federally provided trailer park? Do you have enough drinking water and food? How safe do you feel? What is the distance to the nearest health facility? Since the hurricane, has there been a two-week period when you felt down, depressed or hopeless nearly every day?

Aid workers in conflict-stricken developing countries will not find such data collection questions unusual. But, to be gathering such data in the United States of America is surreal. For all intents and purposes, Robert is an internally displaced person, no different than the IDPs forced from their villages in Sudan, Sri Lanka, or Congo. Most aid agencies voluntarily subscribe to a set of humanitarian minimum standards for their international response efforts to IDPs and refugees. These standards address food, shelter, water and protection, among other categories. But, until this moment, no other organisation is looking at Robert, and his unlikely contingent, through the lens of emergency aid minimum standards. The United States, one of the world's most powerful countries, surely could not have IDPs, or so goes the popular sentiment.

Robert tells more than the questionnaire requires. Speaking in the halted, hushed fashion of someone who has suffered severe trauma, he tells me how he chose not to evacuate as Katrina came boiling in on the Gulf Coast in August 2005. The roof of his apartment caved in, breaking his back. Unable to move and incapable of signalling for help, he agonised through days without food or water. Eventually a friend rescued him and, after his medical needs were tended to, he received a government-issue travel trailer. Now, nine months after the hurricane, food is of paramount concern. A Baptist church operates a food distribution centre one mile from his trailer park. But without transportation and with limited physical mobility, it is nearly impossible for him to walk to the distribution centre, let alone carry groceries home.

As I listen to Robert's story, I roll the dice of decisions over in my mind. Should I tick the boxes on this questionnaire, get into my crappy sedan and hit the road for the next trailer park, as my job requires? Or, do I break the bounds of neutrality and objectivity by secretly slipping him some groceries? And, if I do pass him some food, how will this help him next week when his cupboards are once again bare? I choose to break the rules. When he answers the door on my subsequent—and last—visit he reaches for the grocery bags with teary eyes.

A few days later I encounter a similar situation in southern Louisiana. An elderly woman in another travel trailer has sparse quantities of food, an inability to prepare meals for herself, and receives rare visits from family members that could otherwise lend a helping hand. She is depressed and huddles in the fetal position on her bed. I disobey the rules again, bringing her food items that can be easily prepared, asking her to never disclose the source of the delivery. I encounter many other IDPs whom I do not know how to help—the man whose travel trailer is seeping formaldehyde from its interior surfaces so effusively that it makes my eyes weep; the woman who is planning to give her unborn child to a cousin upon the baby's birth because she cannot afford its care; the toddler who would later drown in an inviting, sparkling swimming pool.

Ironically, though New Orleans was my home, I escaped Katrina's direct hit. When she kicked the Gulf Coast to its knees, I was visiting IDP camps in Sri Lanka as part of a graduate school course on how best to coordinate large-scale disaster relief operations following natural disasters. Due to New Orleans' temporary closure, protracted state of despair, and its relative instability, my university closed shop for one quarter. I returned to the broken, hobbled Crescent City three months after the storm's landfall and resumed my daily life as a graduate school student. I took a part-time job for an international NGO, collecting the information that brought me to Robert's doorstep. By virtue of collecting this data, I learned that half of the respondents I interviewed met the clinical definition of depression.[1] I sickened at the thought of the hoards of depressed people confined to isolated trailer parks throughout the region, without access to community, transportation, or health care. Moreover, every time I stepped outside the confines of my comfortable, ordered home, I faced   destruction and disarray: houses with collapsed roofs, broken stoplights, abandoned neighborhoods, the street side memorial for a woman left for dead after being stuck by a speeding car during the storm, and searched houses still bearing spray-painted markings indicating the number of dead once inside. Katrina had passed, but her ghost remained.

International emergency response and aid workers employed on foreign soil can buffer themselves from the pain their beneficiaries experience by virtue of understanding that, theoretically, they can board a plane and leave the disaster when they so choose. I had come to understand what it is like, however, to be a root-bound resident of such a scene. New Orleans was my home and this ruin was my surround.

Feeling helpless at witnessing this protracted trauma, all the while facing the pressure of completing a graduate degree and seeking a career to pay a mounting tuition debt, I had unconsciously created my own storm. Insomnia, anxiety, and depression were no longer data entry fields on a questionnaire, but my personal experience. Fortunately, my student health care provided access to a psychologist, one of the few remaining in the city, and medications to aid me through each day and each night. But even this came at a cost. The medications were incredibly expensive for

1. Fifty percent of respondents met criteria for Major Depressive Disorder, more than seven times the U.S. national rate. Since displacement, reported suicides/suicide attempts among respondents were approximately 15 times the state's baseline suicide rates and 79 times the baseline attempt rates.

my meagre grad school budget, and the only sleep aid that did not cause significant side effects was not covered by my insurance. Worse still, I grew dependant on the sleep aid.

My desire to work overseas in a developing country struggling with its own emergency or a natural disaster did not diminish, despite the insomnia, anxiety and depression. If anything, these maladies strengthened my determination to apply the skill set I had acquired through my graduate studies and my real-life experiences. A bone, having healed from a break, is said to be stronger than its unbroken counterpart.

Six months later, I landed the job that launched my international career. I arrived in the dusty village of Tambura, South Sudan, days before Christmas 2006. I delighted in my first sights of Africa: children skilfully riding bikes far too large for them across the wide dirt road, teenagers kicking a soccer ball through the town square, cows making their way home during the golden hour of twilight, entire families promenading after Sunday church services dressed in the same brightly coloured waxy fabric. Mangoes hung from trees, turning from hard green to soft yellow. The dictated timing of my arrival coincided with a holiday standstill. While South Sudan had experienced one of the longest running conflicts in all of Africa, this could not be readily discerned. As far as I could see, there were no bullet-ridden buildings and razed villages. My new colleagues each had a story to tell about their effects of the war on their families, but that was not what they wanted to talk about. They wanted to laugh with abandon, smile broadly with shiny, white teeth, and give each other slapping, happy handshakes at each day's dawn.

Eventually, I exhausted my short supply of sleeping tablets. To my surprise I found I could indeed sleep unaided. My anxiety left, taking depression with it. In their wake arose a renewed purpose and world view. I was among people who had experienced immense tragedy and had survived, culture and psyche intact. New Orleans was still limping, but I saw where it could be one day through the jovial, inextinguishable spirit of the Southern Sudanese. I would follow their cues. And so it was that by moving to one of the most undeveloped countries on the African continent, I had begun to heal.

At the time of writing, South Sudan is the newest country in the world having gained independence from Sudan in July, 2011. Located in East Africa, South Sudan is completely landlocked and surrounded by Sudan to the north, Ethiopia and Kenya to the east, Uganda to the south and the Democratic Republic of Congo and Central African Republic to the west.

The country's independence followed two civil wars fought within Sudan during which an estimated two million people were killed and four million displaced.[1] The second civil war was ended by a peace deal called the Comprehensive Peace Agreement, which codified a five year period (2005-2010) of transition ending with a referendum for southern Sudan, and a separate process for the oil-rich border areas of Abyei, South Kordofan and Blue Nile. In 20011, in a peaceful referendum, the southern Sudanese voted to become an independent country: the Republic of South Sudan.

However, Sudan's decades of civil war took a terrible toll on South Sudan leaving it one of the most under-developed countries in the world. According to South Sudan's National Statistics Bureau, the country—with an area the size of France—has a population of 8.26 million.[2] To serve that population, there are only 120 doctors and 100 nurses in the country.[3] Seventy-five percent of the population is illiterate and half live below the poverty line.[4]

---

1   BBC. "Sudan Profile"; 03 October, 2012. Available from: http://www.bbc.co.uk/news/world-africa-14094995.
2   "South Sudan National Bureau of Statistics Fast Facts". Available from http://ssnbs.org.
3   Reuters. "Special Report: In South Sudan, a state of dependency"; 10 July 2012. Available from http://www.reuters.com/article/2012/07/10/us-south-sudan-aid-idUSBRE86909V20120710.
4   "The World Bank South Sudan Country Data". Available from: http://data.worldbank.org/.country/south-sudan.

Fifty percent of the population has no access to clean water and less than ten percent have sanitation.[5] There are few roads and many of these are impassable during the rainy season. Large parts of the country are land-mined and many areas are subject to severe flooding and outbreaks of diseases such as polio, trypanosomiasis (sleeping sickness), and guinea worm.

Whilst South Sudan's separation from Sudan was largely peaceful there were still challenges, such as what to do for the many thousands of Southern Sudanese in Sudan and Northern Sudanese in the South. Local conflicts also continued in different areas of the new country as well as a conflict in the neighbouring areas of South Kordofan and Blue Nile (parts of Sudan bordering South Sudan).

Many UN agencies and NGOs have been operating in the region since the 1960s. Some were partners under the 1989 Operation Lifeline Sudan, which provided a joint UN/NGO umbrella agreement signed with the Sudan People's Liberation Army and enabling humanitarian relief to be brought into the region.

Today, the international community is working with the newly formed government of South Sudan to address these issues as well as to help provide humanitarian response to ongoing natural disasters, internal conflicts and to support the refugees coming from South Kordofan and Blue Nile.

---

5   Global Water Intelligence. "South Sudan Faces up to its Water Challenge"; March 2011.
Available from: http://www.globalwaterintel.com/archive/12/3/general/south-sudan-faces-its-water-challenge.html.

Students at the Makpandu UNHCR Refugee Settlement in Western Equatoria. In October 2008, thousands of Congolese fleeing violence perpetrated by the LRA crossed into South Sudan to safety at three main UNHCR settlements. As the violence continues in DRC, CAR and South Sudan, new arrivals register with UNHCR weekly. ©Jenn Warren

Birunga, 13, escaped alone from the DRC after his father was killed by the LRA. He was taken in by a Sudanese family and continued his journey by truck with 61 other refugees. UNHCR will place him with a family at the Makpandu site while attempting to locate relatives. ©Jenn Warren

Flora Boringba, 6, plays in the Catholic Church her father, Priest Nomi Gbinzako Joseph, built inside the Ezo UNHCR Refugee Settlement in Western Equatoria, South Sudan. ©Jenn Warren

UNHCR trucks transport Congolese refugees and their possessions to the newly created UNHCR site in Makpandu, South Sudan. The journey from Gangura is only 56 kilometers but takes three hours due to the condition of roads. ©Jenn Warren

Built To Carry Thirteen
Mia Ali

I am four hours into my six hour car journey from one end of the sprawling state to the other. We started late, as usual, the need to fuel and provision our Toyota Land Cruiser taking Wani, the driver, by surprise as it always does. A dozen last-minute errands were suddenly deemed crucially important, and the pulsing sun was high in the sky when we eventually left the compound. We need to reach our destination before dark, so we've skipped lunch and my resulting headache is making me surly. I could make it better by drinking some water, but what goes in must come out, and there's no privacy for a woman at the side of these roads. The occasional bush calls tantalisingly, but the fear of mines overcomes the insistent call of my bladder.

The combination of the heat and the constant jolting of the cratered dirt road is lulling me to sleep, and I fight against the closing of my eyes. It's best to keep alert, in case of an attack. I shift in my seat, trying to keep myself awake, and I wince as I peel my sweaty legs off the vinyl seat.

Out of the open window I can see miles of open scrubland, barren and harsh. The dry, orange dust is everywhere, coating the car, the back of my throat and the inside of my nose with its pervasive, metallic smell. Wani and I ran out of things to say three hours ago, and the only sounds are the noise of the engine and the occasional crackle of the radio.

There are no clouds in the sky—it's the dry season; there will be no clouds for at least another two months. The sun beats down mercilessly on the few animals and people who have to eke out a life in the dirt. Every so often, a village flashes by, breaking the monotony. Children, naked or draped in bedraggled, once-white vests, stand in front of crooked mud huts with pointed grass roofs and stare open-mouthed as we pass. Men and women idle under the shade of a tree, on the ground or, if they're considered important enough, on broken plastic chairs. It's too hot now for any activity, so they sit and watch the goats and chickens scrabbling in the dirt.

The slowing of the Land Cruiser alerts me to the fact that we're approaching a barrier. It might be a pile of dirt or rocks, or perhaps a grubby length of string suspended between two sticks. These obstacles are easily avoided, but it's polite to stop until you're given permission to pass. I squint into the distance and see a man at the side of the road, flagging us down.

There's only one reason someone flags you down at one of these barriers, and that's to get a lift. And who can blame them, in this country where only the privileged few have cars? A villager might be lucky and get a lift in a minibus taxi or a passing car, but the likelihood of breaking down in these ancient relics, totally unsuited for the terrain, is high. In contrast, numerous well-maintained NGO 4x4s sail past, one or two staff inside a car built to carry thirteen.

But they rarely stop. I rarely stop. I'm too busy helping beneficiaries to help the people by the side of the road. I comfort myself with the fact that I'm not allowed to, for security reasons. What if the car is in an accident and the passenger gets hurt? What if you inadvertently pick up someone who is persecuting the people you're supposed to be helping? What if your car is commandeered at gunpoint? What if?

So we leave them at the side of the road, in the blazing sun, no way to get where they're trying to go. How many people have I left, I wonder? What do they think of my organisation? I know what they think of me. I see it in their eyes as I explain I'm sorry, it's a question of insurance, if it was my choice, but my hands are tied. Their hopeful smiles fade; they look down, spit on the floor, and turn away even as I speak. Some have raged—more than once we've made a quick and nervous getaway while a drunken soldier rants and waves his gun around, eyes hidden behind dark sunglasses. Because even the soldiers can't get transport here; the destitute army can't pay their wages, much less move them round the country. They seem to have no problem arming them, though.

Wani is muttering under his breath, his eyes on the small group that has now gathered at the side of the road in the distance. I surreptitiously lean on the door lock with my elbow, clicking it into place. I glance over my shoulder, making sure that the lock on the back door is down. On one of my early missions, I made the mistake of not locking the doors. The first time we stopped at a village, twelve people clambered in uninvited and it took us half an hour to get them out again.

There have been times when I've not been able to refuse. Times when I've been senior enough, in a small organisation with less stringent rules. There was the wizened old lady, sitting in the scorching midday sun by the side of a large, muddy lake in the middle of the road. Cars that hadn't made it through the mud lay scattered around like broken teeth, some teetering on two wheels, other nose deep in the murky water, engines flooded. How long she had been stuck there, I didn't know, but I did know she'd be stuck there for hours, possibly days, if I didn't give her a lift. Her grandsons begged me to take her, not asking for themselves. I think this is what persuaded me in the end. She didn't speak English, and she and my driver had no common language. I insisted that she sat in the front and spent the next three hours in a mimed battle of wills over whether she would wear her seatbelt. We came off the road twice, branches from the bushes crowding the road whipping in through her open window. After a backward pirouette through another water-filled hole in the road, she finally agreed to wear the belt, hooked loosely over her right arm. When we reached our destination, she scuttled out of the car and disappeared into the bush without a backward glance. Remembering her ancient face, I wondered what would have happened if we had crashed and she had been injured. What kind of trouble would I have been in? Roadside beatings were not uncommon at crash sites. I didn't give any more lifts after that.

We're approaching the group by the side of the road now. Behind them is a low concrete building surrounded by trees. We roll slowly past a sign:

Primary Health Care Unit
Built with USAID Funding
From the American People

I idly wonder what the American People would think of coming to this clinic. Wani's face is solemn as we pull up. He clearly has an idea what's going on, and I could ask him to explain. But I'm tired and hot, and I don't have the energy to deal with this. With any luck, the group won't speak English and they can explain their issue to Wani, who can rebuff them for me. I force a bright smile as a tall, well-rounded man in cheap suit trousers and a shirt approaches my side of the car. There was once a time I would have started this exchange by asking what he wanted. I long ago realised that nothing could get done until the pleasantries had been completed.

"Good Afternoon, Madam!" His face is pleasant and his expression hopeful.

"Good Afternoon!" I reply. "How are you?"

"I am fine, Madam, thank you for asking. And how are you?"

"I'm good, thank you."

I wait as he greets Wani in a local dialect. Unfortunately, after a brief moment, he turns back to me. I suppress a sigh.

"Madam, I am Simon, the Community Health Worker for this clinic." He gestures behind him at the squat concrete block, no bigger than the reception of my doctor at home. Two splintered wooden benches outside the doorway constitute the waiting room, shaded for at least some of the day by an acacia tree. I know that inside, the unpainted concrete walls will hold a couple of fading, curled posters secured with browning tape.

Do Not Get Sick! Wash With Soap!

Condoms - Put On Your Boots Before You Score!

There will be a peeling wooden desk and a couple of dirty plastic chairs, one for the Community Health Worker and one for the patient. Anyone who comes with the patient will have to stand. An ancient examination couch will be tucked in the corner. The clinic's store of drugs, such as it is, will be held in a metal filing cabinet. There might be a dusty fan on the floor, positioned to give the Community Health Worker and his patient some comfort. But it will never have worked—there is no electricity here. Perhaps patient records are kept—if so, they'll be handwritten and filed on the bookshelf behind the desk. But nobody ever asks for this information, and patients rarely come back for follow up appointments. So maybe they don't waste their time keeping records here.

"A lady is here, with her children," says Simon. Again, he gestures behind him, but my view is blocked by a cluster of people. "She has brought her son here; he was sick with malaria." He looks at his shoes and shakes his head. "She should have brought him many days ago, when he started to get sick. She went to the witchdoctor and he told her not to come." He meets my eyes again. "She is not educated," he explains. He looks into the distance and my eyes follow his gaze, squinting into the glare of the sun. "She walked here this morning, it took them many hours. By the time he got here, he was vomiting badly." He leans into the window, and I flinch backwards from his expression. "I tried to give him medicine, but he couldn't keep it down. He needed the injection, but we ran out of supplies many months ago." He rocks back on his heels, silent. I wait for a moment, but it seems he has finished. I turn to Wani, confused. He looks down at his hands, and not for the first time I feel his embarrassment at my ignorance; at having to explain the obvious to me.

"The boy is dead," Wani says.

A fly is buzzing behind my head, and as I listen to it, I start to hear other sounds. The low babble of voices. A crying child. A woman, wailing. I don't want to turn back to the window. I lower my voice.

"What can we do?" I ask. Wani shrugs. What can we do, indeed. What can we do in this vast, sprawling country, where our money, our time, our efforts are absorbed like a rain drop in the dry season. We push the futility of it all to the back of our minds by making ourselves busy, always planning, reporting, emailing, meeting, driving past people by the side of the road. Nothing we've done has helped this woman, who has lost her child in this barren place for want of a simple and inexpensive injection.

"Does she need a lift?" I ask Wani. He won't meet my eyes. He knows that this is forbidden by our organisation, and he knows that the choice - and the consequence - is mine.

"Does she?" I ask again. He nods, still not looking at me.

I turn back to the window. I can see her now, sitting on the splintered wooden bench, head bent over a bundle in a white cloth, which she clutches to her chest as she rocks back and forth.

"Where does she need to go?" I ask Simon. He is taken aback for a moment. He must have been expecting me to make my excuses. The thought makes me feel ashamed. Ashamed for all the times I've made them.

The woman climbs into the back of the Land Cruiser and Simon passes her the white bundle. I can see the boy now - he looks about two, the same age as my sister's youngest, although he could be older; children here are malnourished and tend to be small for their age. He looks like he is sleeping, and I can't tear my eyes away from him. His mother is still wailing as Simon helps her daughter, who looks about six, up into the car. She is holding a baby girl, and shoots shy glances at me. I smile at her, and her gaze darts away. Simon climbs in and we set off, Wani staring ahead at the road, his expression grim. I sense his disapproval but I don't understand it.

"Our clinic is supported by the government," says Simon. "We haven't had a drugs delivery for six months and we haven't been paid for the last three. I will continue to work until the supplies run out. After that..." He shrugs. "We don't have any transport. I try to get to the communities whenever I can, to teach them about sanitation, and common diseases. But they prefer to go to their village witchdoctor; they don't trust Western medicine." He gestures towards the woman, who is keening loudly. "They come to us when it's too late, and then they blame us for the deaths of their children." He turns and barks a local word at the woman, who immediately stops her wail and starts to rock and hum as tears stream down her cheeks.

"It's ok!" I say, "Leave her be." Simon looks at me, the friendliness gone from his eyes. He starts talking to the woman in a language I don't understand. There are around two hundred local languages - it didn't seem worth learning just one. His tone is harsh, and the woman shrinks backwards into the seat. Wani joins in. I look from one to the other. Wani sounds angry.

"What's going on?" I ask him. He looks at me, then back at the road.

"We are telling her that she should have brought her son to the clinic earlier. Then he would not be dead."

For a moment, I wonder if I've heard him right. This woman, who lost her son less than thirty minutes ago, is being told that it is all her fault. How could anyone say such a thing to a grieving mother? I should defend her, but the faces of the two men look hard and alien and my courage fails me. I look at her, wishing there was something I could do to comfort her. Wishing I had learnt at least one language. She is still rocking, rearranging the white cloth around her son's head, which flops backwards across her arm.

Death is common in this country, where a girl is more likely to die in childbirth than to finish primary school. But most of the time, I can treat it like an abstract concept. I can pretend that mothers here don't feel the death of a child like mothers back home. I wonder how my sister would feel if she lost one of her girls. I wonder how she'd feel if someone told her it was her fault; I wonder how her other children would feel. The baby starts to cry, and her elder sister shushes her expertly.

We are approaching a village now, and people are emerging from the trees and huts to meet us. As the woman gets down from the car, her keening resumes and other voices join hers. A tall man in tattered shorts and a thin, buttonless shirt takes the dead boy from her arms. He doesn't speak and his face is resigned as they walk away together, untouching.

The girl, forgotten, climbs down with the baby. I don't want this to be her life. I search for something to give her, and find a shawl that I brought from home. I hand it to her, and she takes it, confused. Then she is gone. In the months and years to come, I will imagine her wearing it at school, her head bent over her books, or laughing with her friends.

Wani and I are left on the road, watching the backs of the villagers as they disappear into the trees. There is nothing more for us to do here.

We drive on in our empty car, built to carry thirteen.

Falling Down
Steph Roberson

It was late June 2009, and I had been in Juba, South Sudan, for eight weeks. Although I had lived and worked abroad for many years in South Korea, Kuwait, and Nepal, this was my first trip to a post-conflict country, working specifically for a NGO. I was conducting research on the impacts of road construction on local communities as part of my Masters degree, as well as collecting data to help refugees returning to South Sudan reintegrate into their communities.

Despite the prosaic-sounding nature of the topic, it was exciting, fascinating, and interesting work, travelling around the state of Central Equatoria talking with communities, holding focus group discussions, conducting interviews, and running training sessions. Although the climate was hot and humid, the landscape was fresh, green and beautiful, nothing like the bleak desert landscapes my friends had imagined when I first told them I would be going to South Sudan.

I spent most of my evenings in my room on the NGO compound, reading or watching TV on my laptop. The compound consisted of a collection of bedrooms, communal kitchen and toilet/shower blocks where the international staff lived, as well as the offices we worked in every day. The whole compound was surrounded by a high wall and protected by security guards day and night. The office building had the luxury of an air conditioning unit, but the bedrooms had only large, ancient ceiling fans to battle valiantly if ineffectually against the hot, sticky nights. As the power in Juba was sporadic at best, there was a generator that ran on diesel fuel during the day to power the computers, lights, air conditioning, and to charge up the huge industrial batteries, which provided back-up power overnight. It would be too wasteful to run the generator all night, as fuel was expensive and sometimes not available at all. The batteries in theory should have provided enough charge for the lights and ceiling fans in the bedrooms to last all night, but in reality they frequently ran down at around 3am or 4am, leaving us tossing and turning, sweating into our mattresses until the generator started up again at 7am.

I travelled south to Kajo Keji, and spent a couple of fun evenings with a rough-and-ready road construction crew, pounding beers and shamelessly enjoying their air conditioning and the excuse to use as many dirty words as I could think of. I was captivated by the landscape, the round tukul huts made of mud and straw, the gazelles and deer I saw in abundance, the large baboons racing up and down boulders, the lush greenness of it all, being so close to the enormous lazy expanse of the Nile.

Back in Juba I had also been to a few parties at the landmine NGO's compound—mainly big, burly South African and Zimbabwean ex-military men, who knew how to drink and have more fun than anyone else I have ever met. Considering the incredibly dangerous and risky nature of their work, searching for and attempting to safely remove landmines and unexploded ordinances, I wasn't surprised that they partied so hard.

I spent my weeks in South Sudan talking with communities about their experiences of returning home after living for years in exile as refugees, trying to understand their needs and identify activities that we could offer to help them. The NGO I was working for mainly focused on livelihoods and reintegration activities, such as offering returned refugees training courses in carpentry, sewing, baking, and farming, and providing them with seeds, tools, equipment and financial support for their businesses. I was also meeting and interviewing staff from other NGOs, and various UN branches, and I had collected a lot of research and needs assessment data, and was nearly done finalising my report.

During my time there, I experienced a couple of security incidents that had brought home to me the dangers inherent in the work that we do. On one occasion, heading back to Juba after visiting a village to collect needs assessment data, our drivers were forced to pull over by the roadside after a Sudanese military vehicle stopped us and told us that bandits only half a kilometre ahead of us had shot a lorry driver to steal his goods. We had to make some quick decisions about the best course of action for the safety of our whole team; to turn back and head for the village we had just left, and risk more bandits on the road now that darkness was fast approaching: to spend the night in our two Toyota Land Cruisers by the roadside and hope we were safe there; or to wait for any passing traffic to help us and continue on to Juba, risking bandits on the road ahead. Luckily we soon saw a convoy of World Health Organisation vehicles and were able to travel safely back to Juba with them.

On another occasion, we had just stopped our vehicle at a military checkpoint, when one of our staff members jumped out of the car to buy some mangoes at the roadside, as they were cheaper in the villages than back in Juba. As soon as he got out of the car, an armed and very drunk soldier entered our vehicle and demanded that we drive him to his base, 10 kilometres away. In spite of our stance as an impartial NGO with a very clear policy on carrying arms and soldiers in our cars, we could not persuade him to get out of the car. We spent over 40 minutes politely asking that he exit the vehicle, conscious that he was drunk, and armed, and we did not want to make him angry. Once again, as the sun started to set and the dangers of being out on the roads after dark became more pressing, we were forced to compromise. We would take him to his base if he agreed to remove all of the ammunition from his rifle.

In spite of these incidents, I had always managed to get back to the compound safely and, in general, the security situation in South Sudan at that time was very stable, especially in Juba.

The only mild traumas I suffered during my stay were from the terror of the over-sized cockroaches that infested the toilets, and one night when I accidentally trod on and squashed a large frog as I made my way through the dark to the toilet blocks.

In my final week before flying home, I was asked to move from my room in the compound into the director's bedroom due to a shortage of space. Several new staff members had arrived and needed rooms and, as I was leaving soon anyway, the director had gone to stay with his fiancée on a nearby compound for a few days, to help free up some space.

Like my previous room, there was no air-conditioning in the director's room, just a heavy-duty ceiling fan that lazily moved the muggy air from one part of the room to another. The large double bed had a wooden frame raised above it on posts, like a four-poster bed, to keep the mosquito net suspended above it, so that it didn't touch you as you slept.

It was late on Saturday night, and the weather was sweltering, still close to 30 degrees, even at midnight. It was humid and close, with no breeze at all, other than the faint movement of air that the fan was able to muster. I was sitting up in bed under the mosquito net, the rickety fan turned up to full power, my chin resting on my knees, watching old re-runs of American sitcoms on my laptop.

Suddenly there was an incredibly loud and powerful bang, and I instinctively cowered and threw my arms above my head to protect myself. I could feel things falling down on me, bouncing off my legs and the bed, and I could feel the mosquito net drop down over me, closing in on my arms and head. My first thought was that a bomb had gone off and that the ceiling was caving in. Once things stopped falling and the room fell silent, I slowly opened my eyes and looked up at the ceiling directly above the bed.

It was completely intact. No damage at all, not even a crack in the plaster. I looked at the bed in confusion, still tangled up in the mosquito net, at the shattered chunks of wood lying all over the sheets and across my legs, and looked up again. The wooden frame around the bed, which had been holding up the mosquito net, was in pieces. There were big chunks of wood lying all over the place, twisted in the collapsed net, and a large splintered two-by-four hung at a crazy angle from the remaining upright post.

I looked around in consternation, trying to figure out what had caused the explosion, and destroyed the wooden frame around my bed, when I suddenly saw it on the floor, less than a foot from me in a crumpled heap of twisted metal beside the bed. The ceiling fan.

I looked at it in shock for a minute, and then, realising what had happened, started frantically feeling my legs to make sure they were both still attached and uninjured. Horrified, I realised that in order for the fan to get to that side of the bed, it must have snapped off the ceiling at full speed, sheared through several sturdy planks of wood, and shot right across the bed where my legs should have been, had I been lying down asleep rather than curled up watching TV.

As it slowly sank in to my consciousness that I was by some miracle completely unharmed, I realised that watching TV had probably saved my legs, if not my life. Had I been lying down asleep, the blades of that heavy metal fan would have hit my legs at considerable speed, and most likely broken both of them, at the very least. If it could shear through a two-by-four plank of wood that quickly and cleanly, I imagine it would have cut straight through my legs like butter.

I sat there for a minute, absorbing the absurdity of it all. I had spent months reassuring my family that South Sudan would be ok, and I would not be travelling anywhere too unsafe or insecure, and yet I just had an extremely frightening near-death experience while safe and alone in my bedroom. I had survived drunken soldiers waving guns in my face, bandits on the roads, cockroaches and frogs, only to be almost killed by a poorly-installed ceiling fan.

Figuring that I'd better clean up the mess I got out of bed, and started picking up large pieces of wood and then something occurred to me. No one would believe what had just happened. It was too unusual and surreal and, still slightly dazed, I was convinced that if I cleared it all up before anyone saw it, they might think I had somehow destroyed the bed myself. The director's bed no less.

I needed a witness. I rushed out of the room into the compound to try and find the night security guard, or someone who could at least bear witness to this bizarre incident before I cleaned it all up. Halfway across the compound I bumped into our new logistician, who had just arrived two days earlier from Kenya, and was headed across the compound to the toilet blocks.

"Oh thank God! Please could you come to my room? I just need you to see something, really quickly" I babbled, rushing ahead of him back to the room, "You'll never believe it, it's crazy! Seriously, it's totally bizarre! Just come to my room for a minute."

To be approached in the middle of the night by a mildly hysterical woman in her nightgown who insisted that he come to her bedroom immediately for an unspecified reason must have seemed pretty peculiar, especially to a new staff member barely two days into the job. To his credit, however, he followed me, albeit hesitantly, looking extremely uncomfortable and nervous.

I stood in the doorway and gestured triumphantly at the chaotic scene. "There! Look! You see?"

He stood for a second, confused, and then, slowly, as he understood what had happened, a concerned look dawned across his face.

"Oh my God! Are you alright? Are you hurt?"

"No, no, don't worry, I'm fine. Really. But do you see what happened? With the fan? It's crazy isn't it?"

He surveyed the damage again, looked thoughtfully up at the ceiling where the fan used to be, marched across the room, plucked the offending heap of metal off the floor, and carried it outside. As he walked past me, he paused, and said "Don't worry, ma'am, I'll fetch you another fan."

That made me laugh, in spite of everything. Logisticians tend to be very practical people, and I found it hilarious that after seeing the destruction wrought by a ceiling fan, and ensuring that I was ok, his immediate response was to procure me another fan, so that I would be able to sleep through the night comfortably!

Later, after we had cleared away the mess, and he had returned and installed a smaller, standing fan next to the bed, he looked thoughtfully around the room and said, "You know, I think maybe tomorrow I will check all the other fans on the compound."

Beating The Odds
Tracy O'Heir

Five years into my career as a social worker, I needed a change. I am not sure what kind of change I thought I would get by moving to work in Nimule, Sudan in 2002. A 20-year civil war between the Government of Sudan and rebel Sudanese People's Liberation Army (SPLA) had been stopped by a fragile ceasefire that was still holding when I arrived. I had no idea what I was getting myself into and, had I known, I probably would never have shown up at all. I decided to spend two years living and working in one of the areas under the control of the SPLA—a temporary home to tens of thousands of people forced to flee their villages due to the war raging all over the southern third of the country.

I was working as a volunteer for an NGO as the administrator for the school system in the area, which was comprised of a few counties along the border. Our neck of the woods was relatively peaceful. The front line of the Sudanese war was far enough away that it had little effect on our daily lives. Sadly, however, another armed group operated in the area and posed a great danger to all—The Lord's Resistance Army (LRA). The LRA was a combination cult/militia/ group of armed bandits, under the leadership of Joseph Kony. At the time, the LRA would roam the rural areas of Northern Uganda and Southern Sudan, kidnapping children, mutilating women and men, stealing what they needed to survive.

I spent my days figuring out how to get textbooks, food for school lunches, and teachers' salaries from the nearest town in Uganda, across the Nile and to the schools, some of which were another 30 miles away, all the while avoiding attacks by the LRA. Then I had to figure out how to keep those things safe once I got them there.

While this work was challenging, it reinforced what I had come to believe so well: that I was ill-suited to accompany people through their problems at home in Chicago. It had become clear that I could not take the problems of, for example, a 14-year old high school student in Chicago seriously, when I knew a little bit about the problems a 14-year old high school student in Southern Sudan faced. Simply surviving, not having to get married, flee as a refugee, or work to support the family by the 9th grade was an act of sheer determination and an accomplishment in and of itself. Most Southern Sudanese were lucky if they had the resources to make attendance at school feasible and to live in a place where they could gather in the shade of some trees to learn, where the war and the LRA did not make it too dangerous to gather together. School was considered a luxury after a student's family had food and was safe. And for girls, even more so. According to UNICEF, less than one percent of girls in South Sudan finish primary school— and the ones that do are more likely to be married than graduate.

I arrived in Nimule in July, and at Christmas that year, I volunteered to stay during the holidays and mind the compound and offices where I lived and worked. My colleagues, all Southern Sudanese, spent the holidays with their families in refugee camps in Uganda, Ethiopia, Kenya, or in other parts of Southern Sudan. It was the first time I ever spent Christmas away from my family and I did it in style.

I remember that Christmas as one of the few times that I really felt truly comfortable and at home there. Only later have I also come to think of it as a time when I was horribly naïve about what was happening around me. At the time, I was simply won over by the celebration and relaxation of my first Christmas in the hot, dry season that December brings to Southern Sudan.

On Christmas day, I was invited to a few different homes of co-workers and friends who lived in the area. Nimule is set on a hill, overlooking the Nile. At that time, the town was small and I spent the day walking from house to house visiting, eating and drinking. The final visit of the day was to the home of the woman who worked as a cook in our compound. The only way she would agree to take the day off was if I agreed to come to her house for dinner.

Another friend was invited, a Ugandan woman, who served as a nurse in our town's only medical facility, a clinic run by the Catholic church. We made the trek up the hill to her home about a mile outside of the main town, in the 'new' area of Nimule where homes had started popping up after the SPLA managed to secure the town from the LRA.

We didn't have a car, but a friend who worked for another NGO promised to stop by and give us a lift back to town. We enjoyed our dinner, some drinks, and dessert, played with the kids, and I especially enjoyed it as one of the few times I was in the company of other women who were not there to serve others but to celebrate.

As it got later and later, however, our friend didn't show up to give us a lift. We were wondering what to do. It was too dangerous to walk home alone, two women alone at night in an area where everyone had an automatic weapon and the LRA may be lurking somewhere nearby. As night fell, we stood by the road with our host and waited for anyone to drive by - there were only 10 or 11 cars in the whole town, so we were bound to know the driver of the next car no matter who they were. We waited about an hour and then saw in the distance a car speeding up the dirt road, lights set on bright, blinding us as it pulled up.

It was an NGO car and in the passenger seat was a man from the SPLA with his AK-47 on his lap. Many NGOs will not allow armed people in their cars, not only in South Sudan but anywhere that they work—as a way of maintaining neutrality and making themselves available to provide services to anyone in need of lifesaving assistance, no matter what side of a conflict they may be on. This particular NGO normally stuck to this rule, so I knew something was wrong.

The driver, head of office for the NGO and a good friend, came to a sliding, screeching halt in the dirt track and yelled, "Get in, get in right now, hurry!" No time to think, we quickly said our goodbyes and scurried into the Land Cruiser, which immediately took off—in the wrong direction. And, as the car started moving, I noticed a very drunk woman in the back.

As soon as we pulled away our friend who was driving told us the story. A pregnant woman just a little bit further up the road had been in labor at home all day long, and word was sent to the Nimule hospital that that there was a problem. I never really did know how my friend and his SPLA companion got involved, but the doctor was nowhere to be found so these two guys found the best health worker available at that moment—a local midwife who was drunk as could be.

We headed out to find the woman in labour. We soon got close to where this woman's home was meant to be, but we could not find it. The only one who really knew the way was the midwife and, in her condition, she couldn't find it. Finally, the pregnant woman's family hailed to us. It was clear now that the midwife would not be much help but, luckily, my companion was an experienced nurse.

The family led us to their home and we arrived to hear screaming from inside a tukul—the typical round mud huts with thatched roofs in which most Southern Sudanese live. The nurse jumped out of the car and ran in, only to run back out seconds later. We would have to take this woman to the hospital immediately. She was delivering twins, the first of which was stuck in the birth canal and coming out arm first.

While she was still relaying this to us the woman giving birth was carried out of her tukul and quickly loaded into the back of our car, screaming in pain with every movement. I scrambled out of the way to make room as they laid her in the vehicle that already had several of the seats removed, as it was normally used to haul equipment and medicine.

The nurse sat down on the floor of the car next to her and murmured to her in Madi, the local language. As the car started and lurched forward, the woman's hand shot up and seized onto mine, squeezing tightly with every bump in the road. She was so cold despite the fact that she was sweating and it was quite hot outside. About half way into town she fainted.

Around that time we also passed the home of a local official who flagged us down warning us against entering town. While the Southern Sudanese were united against the Government of Sudan, they were quite divided along tribal lines among themselves. That Christmas evening, a disagreement had degenerated into tribal fighting with gunshots, rocks, and bricks being hurled around in the centre of town. But, we couldn't go back, so we forged ahead. We had no choice.

We pulled into the dark grounds of the hospital and a tall South Sudanese man emerged from the dark buildings. He was a nursing assistant and explained that the hospital was out of fuel for the generator and that the only other person on duty that night—in the whole hospital—was a nurse. Everyone else was out celebrating the holiday.

The woman was quickly unloaded from the car and the pain of movement woke her up. The woman and the nurses disappeared into the dark hospital, leaving me alone with the driver and his armed passenger. After six months in Nimule I had no reason to be afraid—the SPLA were the best protection I had against so many other dangers—and this person in particular was someone I had seen around town many times before.

After a brief discussion, we decided to try to find a way to get some lights on in the hospital and, after a futile visit to the owners of the two shops that sold fuel in the town, we settled on candles from the one shop owner we could find. We bought all the candles he had—about 20—and some matches, rushed back over to the hospital and handed them over to the nursing assistant.

And then we sat there looking at each other. The others in the car wanted to take me home—with everything going on they felt it was safest for me to be back in my home compound with our guard. I agreed. I was dropped off and they returned to the hospital in case anything else was needed. Although for years after, I have wondered what they would have done in the middle of the night if action was needed. Where would they have gone? The nearest accessible hospital with a doctor and electricity was in Gulu, Uganda, a five hour drive away through some very dangerous territory.

At home I dropped into bed and fell asleep immediately. I woke with a start six hours later. Jumping up, I threw my clothes on and started the walk up the hill to the hospital. As I got closer, I was asking myself, what am I rushing towards exactly? According to UNDP, South Sudan has the highest maternal mortality rate in the world—2,054 per 100,000 live births. This is an astronomical figure representing a 1 in 7 chance of a woman dying during her lifetime from pregnancy related causes. But I wasn't thinking about statistics. I had been in South Sudan six months and knew how many women died during childbirth. I assumed that the mother and the babies had died in the night but I hoped not and had to know for sure.

I arrived at the hospital to find nothing short of a Christmas miracle. The guard at the gate informed me that the woman and one of the twins had survived. Overcome with excitement, and more than a little shocked, I didn't even say hello. I rushed out to the market and bought some fresh food for the new mother.

Upon returning, I headed straight to the maternity ward, a sparse, moldy, crumbling building, with 30 beds and no electricity, where patients' families have to supply bed sheets and food for their hospitalised family members.

There she was—exhausted and holding her baby. Our communication was limited at best. In fact, we could not speak to each other at all, having no language in common and no one to translate. But that did not matter. That morning sitting there in silence eating bananas and holding hands with a woman I barely knew, as she held her baby, I knew I had witnessed something incredible—both mother and baby had beaten the odds. That was better than any present I could have imagined.

I can't even remember what the big deal was.

Maybe it was some error in the stock count. My warehouse manager, a reasonably friendly and easy-going guy, seemed to be holding things up. All I remember is how I roared at him. How we ended up facing off against one another. How I slammed my fist on the plastic table overflowing with dusty paper and nearly toppled the computer. How the loud industrial fan behind us was blowing hot air in our faces. How sweaty and smelly we were. How we glared at each other as if our lives depended on this issue. How incompetent, insolent and utterly unhelpful I felt he was being in that moment. How I almost hit him. That's how angry I was. How futile my efforts were to get, well, anything done in this place, and how he was just another contributing factor to a litany of challenges: broken down vehicles, bureaucratic hurdles to firing people, extortion, and the pending monsoon season to name a few.

I stormed out of the warehouse, making my way over to the living quarters, and cowered and howled behind the latrines. I had done my best to adopt a fusion of ruthless efficiency and hakuna matata, and it felt like the result was one scratchy, cynical, impatient bitch. I had a shorter temper, thinner patience. and almost any trace of compassion had been dutifully packed away in a proverbial closet. I took my cue from the other, more experienced expatriates around me. Compassion was for sissies, or at best, something the communications department needed in order to raise funds. Trying to connect with others, especially local staff, was considered, at best, chummy and cliché. We were being paid to be on call 24/7 for twelve weeks at a time, not to flinch at the paradoxes, not to get too attached. We were there to just get on with the job.

I passed the workaholic element with flying colours. Productivity was the name of my game; I was, after all, a logistician of sorts. If only everyone else could just be a bit more organised, well then, the world would be swell.

However, I never quite got the hang of the whole detached approach, of, consciously or not, setting oneself adrift from any community, at home or on mission. My heart winced whenever I met someone who seemed all too happy to have thoroughly unmoored themselves as such, and some no longer even in the name of the humanitarian imperative. The colleague who insisted he wasn't here to 'save babies and all that shit' and thought, instead, that I'd appreciate his comparison of the quality of prostitutes in Bangkok to Bamako. Or, the co-worker who nonchalantly told me she simply didn't want to go home at the end of her mission—she preferred life in the bush. Or, the one who 'forgot to mention', for more than a year, that he was in fact married. Or, the other who prided himself on starting out in the Bosnian war and, decades later, was looking for a retirement gig where he could be left alone and far from his family. Or, the gutless wonder who did a runner when his holiday came around, leaving staff and programmes without warning, planning, or remorse.

While it would be idealistic to suggest that the local staff with whom I worked were always brimming with integrity, they rarely got such opportunities to compartmentalise their lives. Their social fabric fastened them to a particular community which meant, at the very least, they were more likely to try to leave a trail of good relationships behind them.

As expatriates, we can be tempted by the illusion that detachment automatically equals freedom, and that freedom automatically equals life satisfaction. Yet, there's that persistent sinking feeling of isolation or loneliness at times. How often do we try to squash it with more work or more drink, or whatever short-term fix we think will do the trick? Why is all this freedom not quite what it was cracked up to be?

In the meantime, each weekend, the warehouse manager would head back to his village, to his family, to a community. Whether he leaned on them, soaking up the quasi-heroic status of being gainfully employed by the South Sudanese equivalent of Price Waterhouse Coopers, or they leaned on him, enjoying the precarious upward mobility brought by an international NGO salary, they had each other to invest in.

What I lacked, such that I found myself cowering behind the latrines, was the sense of real community and real relationships—face-to-face people to trust, people to hold me accountable, people to lean on. There's something to be said for remembering that we are social, relational beings and that the most real relationships are those that persist through life's ups and downs. It took me a while to notice, but I suspect it was blindingly obvious to the local staff around me. Their social fabric must have seemed some worthy compensation for the insecurity that life presented them day after day. How bizarre it must have been that we, the expatriates, would forfeit our own natural environment and longstanding relationships to insert ourselves, usefully or otherwise, into their relatively insecure world.

More than a few times I saw expatriate colleagues brush off the local staff's well-intended questions regarding our families, our villages, our 'normal' lives, back home. Our blithe responses were met with bemused reactions: local staff screwing up their noses and tilting their heads to the side in incomprehension. This notion of periodically bouncing around the world to help people we'd never met (especially if we'd let slip that we could be earning 'so much more' back home), must have seemed so foreign and illogical. For many of them, the purpose of their job was primarily in order to support their community, to enjoy a life filled with good relationships. They worked to live, not lived to work. What could possibly be more important to us than our own families and our own communities?

However, the expatriate aid worker lifestyle is well set up to lull us into a sense that the work we do is so damn important that we have to sacrifice everything for it—most especially friendship, relationship, and community. We put in long hours in remote locations, in very foreign cultures, where our own rules and protocols set us apart as the other. We live and socialise with a random group of international colleagues who are somewhat free to reinvent themselves with each new mission. We spend our year coming and going on regular R'n'R cycles to exotic holiday destinations before we go for good, as quickly as we came. And we start to think this is perfectly normal.

In theory, through this process we're giving of ourselves to someone—the beneficiaries. In reality, we give ourselves to something, usually built on numbers—dollars, households, tonnage, coverage—or less quantifiable notions such as behaviour change, empowerment, and social cohesion (of beneficiaries). The risk we run is to forget entirely about the someones around us and the someones we left behind, in the bid to efficiently strive for the something.

The more time I spend in the field, the more convinced I become that dispensing of relationships—real relationships—with those around us, in the name of the transitory nature of humanitarian work, is one of the biggest hindrances to achieving results—and it is not doing a lot of good for us as individual expatriate aid workers either. Nothing can substitute for real life, face-to-face encounters.

Where do we start to try and get closer to authentic encounters in the face of such transient work? It's not always big things. To me it's the simple things, like spending evenings at the bedside of my administrative assistant in Congo for the weeks after she miscarried her baby. Or knowing that by keeping that older man on as a guard I can help him feed his orphaned granddaughter. It's seeing a junior guard conducting the choir with flair at the tiny mud-brick church in the village on a Sunday morning. It's being able to give our housekeeper a job as well as a chance to learn to read and write. It's being able to recognise someone's talent and effort and reward them for it. It's celebrating when the fleet manager becomes a dad for the first time. It's being told, "Lucy, you're the only boss we've had who seems to care about who we are—who cares about the whole of us." It's building trust, having that trust betrayed, and rebuilding trust again. It's about recognising that we're not completely autonomous, no matter how much Western culture may idolise this notion. We're social beings, and I think if we're honest with ourselves, we're looking for authentic social encounters.

That authenticity comes from recognising that we'll never be just the 'giver'. We have to learn to be humble and grateful receivers. I'm constantly learning how to do this. Having all my Muslim team there to celebrate Easter when my plans to get home were foiled by an untimely bomb blast. Being taken on a wild boat ride for a birthday present. Finding they went the extra mile, because it was for me. Seeing someone who had a tendency to be antagonistic stop giving me a hard time because they know, well, I give a damn about them. Having them give a damn about me. Seeing people grow right in front of your eyes—and seeing how they can help you grow too. It's not the show-stopping things or the statistics that you find in donor reports but it is the little things, the ordinary, daily gifts of ourselves to each other that leave us changed, for better or worse.

Still, as precious as those experiences are, I also recognise that they're no match for the lifelong value of family and longstanding friends who know me through and through. Why is it that a lot of us, after a few years, are keen to settle for life in a capital city, to find a significant other, even start a family? Is it that we weren't truly committed to the cause from the start? Is it that we're just attracted to the nice, comfortable lifestyle but wanted a little adventure tourism first? I don't think so.

For most of us in aid work, I believe that we end up starving, after years of a transitory lifestyle, for genuine relationship and community. Something stable, somewhere where we can not only unpack more than 23 kilos of luggage, but also have time enough to put down some roots and to unpack more than just the first layer of who we are. We have always wanted to invest ourselves, but the aid work lifestyle prods us to do the opposite, or to do so in a piecemeal and fleeting fashion.

We can start by looking at the relative stability that our local staff often have through their communities and families despite the insecurity or suffering that is going on around them. We need to recognise that this is what we lack, this is the vacuum. I believe that investing in relationships, building trust and reducing the gaping chasm of otherness that is often found between expatriate and national staff is not only going to improve the outcomes for the hundreds, even thousands, of usually nameless and faceless beneficiaries; it is going to leave everyone better off because that's simply being human, recognising our need to give ourselves in relationship and in community.

There isn't some shortcut, be it an institution, a brand, technology, efficiency, or medicine to relieving human suffering on a grand scale that doesn't involve taking a good hard look at how we interact with each other on a small scale—with honesty, integrity, clarity, humour, compassion, gentleness and fairness. Sincere human relations keep us real and grounded. Relieving human suffering starts by recognising each one of us is an end in ourselves. The stock count is only a means to an end. Let's keep the priorities clear.

Haiti
Introduction

Haiti is a country in the Caribbean that shares an island with the Dominican Republic. The country has struggled for decades with political instability, high levels of corruption, crime and environmental degradation that has resulted in economic instability and stifled development. In 2010, it was estimated that 86 percent of people in the capital city, Port au Prince, lived in slums and that half the population had no access to latrines or tap water.[1]

On 12 January 2010, a 7.0 magnitude earthquake struck the capital. An estimated 220,000 people were killed and 300,000 injured.[2] Overnight, approximately 1.5 million people were homeless and 3.5 million were affected across the country. Hundreds of thousands of buildings and infrastructure were destroyed.

Both the Haitian government and the international community attempted to respond but they too had been severely affected. The national palace and key government ministries had been damaged, and an estimated 25 percent of Haitian civil servants had been killed. The building of the United Nations peacekeeping mission had also collapsed, killing many, including the Head of Mission.

Recovery and rehabilitation efforts were still ongoing at the time of writing, with Oxfam reporting that two years after the earthquake over half a million people were still displaced. [3]

---

1   "Haiti Earthquake Facts and Figures". Available from: http://www.dec.org.uk/haiti-earthquake-facts-and-figures.
2   Ibid.
3   "Two years on and Haiti's reconstruction proceeds "at a snail's pace", leaving half a million Haitians homeless". Available from: http://www.oxfam.org/en/pressroom/pressrelease/2012-01-10/two-years-on-haiti-reconstruction-proceeds-snail-pace.

Personal Earthquakes

Alison Hayes

When the phone call came, I was pleased. It had been strange to watch the coverage saturate the news and feel like a by-stander. At Heathrow airport, waiting to board one of the flights open only to emergency response teams, I wandered amongst orange-clad search and rescue teams, petted the dogs trained to detect people trapped under rubble and hoped that my place on one of the overbooked seats was deserved.

The charity I would be working with had been in Haiti for three decades before the 12 January 2010 earthquake that killed more than 200,000 people. As Manager for Policy, Advocacy and Communications, I was going to support the national and international relief effort, assess the humanitarian needs and advocate for them through the organisation's global network.

The airport in the capital, Port-au-Prince had been damaged, so we flew into neighbouring Dominican Republic. I continued overland by bus, downing the vial of oral cholera vaccine that the doctor had yesterday forbidden me to take at the same time as 11 other injections. Beside the bus' wheels milled some of the two million people made homeless overnight: leaving their pancaked city to seek shelter with extended family in the country-side; heading towards the American Embassy to queue under make-shift shade that had to be extended with every passing hour; or simply sitting on the pavement to guard the piles of rubble that remained of their homes.

There is almost no need to describe the scenes in the first days after the quake. No need to repeat the worn-out, inadequate words used to describe suffering on such a massive scale. Port-au-Prince, was 'devastated', 'tragic', 'horrifying'; but words cannot convey how it filled my eyes, nose and ears, how human misery burrowed under my fingernails and slicked greasily over my hair.

Entering our office for the first time, I squeezed around a small desk where several colleagues were already jostling for elbow-room. Our second office building had been severely damaged and was condemned, so the offices had been combined into the building with the stronger structure. Always in search of space, I would sometimes work in the bathroom, alongside another colleague who balanced her laptop on the sink. As I began writing an email in the vain hope that there might be internet later that day, the pens on my desk suddenly clattered up and down and my stomach rose to my throat. A guttural groan came from the belly of the building as the walls and floor strained against each other in different directions. Someone swore and we were on our feet, moving as one panicked group towards the door.

"Stop! Under your desks!" I heard shouted above the noise and I stood gazing around me, caught in the paralysis of split-second decisions that could determine who lived and who died. The week before, a colleague had been killed by falling debris as he ran down the corridor to escape the building.

Silence. As quickly as it had begun, the violent shaking stopped. So passed my first experience of the aftershocks that would plague us at least twice a day for the next month. Over time, I reacted less to the daytime tremors, posting on Facebook with false-bravado as a reassurance to friends, "now able to type through aftershocks!"

Over the next few weeks, damaged houses and offices would be knocked down by yellow cranes swinging wrecking balls. However, in those early days, people could be seen climbing sweatily over the bones of their houses, searching for people and pulling out clothes, pans and anything else that could be salvaged, carrying them away to make-shift camps. More disturbing, to me, than the buildings that had been flattened from three-stories to three-meters high, were those that stood perfectly intact minus an entire wall. These survivors sat obscenely agape, open like doll-houses for the world to stare in at the most private of objects—a family photo hanging crooked on the wall, a refrigerator newly stocked with food that would never be eaten, a young boy's red shorts.

I spent my days talking to the people who crammed into every open space—children, the elderly, women, men and more children. We had to prioritise protection and sanitation for these vulnerable groups. "What do you need? What can we do?" I asked them, over and over and over again.

At the end of each day, we would be driven home before the 6pm curfew and continue meetings in the lounge. That was the convenient upside of living with colleagues. The downside was living with forty of them in a house designed for five, with no running water or flushing toilets. As we queued for the bathroom, clutching buckets of water from the well in the garden, we would hold the nightly debate as to whether it would be safer to sleep inside or in the garden. We all had our own strategies for coping with the aftershocks. After getting repeatedly tangled in my mosquito net when running out of the room in the dark, I went without a net, and stored a water bottle, torch and mobile phone under my pillow in case I could not leave. When I chose to sleep indoors, I would wake in the morning to an eerie outline of my body, created by plaster dust that had been shaken down by tremors.

"I'm more tired in the morning, than when I go to bed the night before," I confided sleepily over coffee to our Haitian Country Director one morning. On the day of the earthquake, she had run home to find her own mother amongst the victims. "How do you manage to keep coming in?" She smiled wanly over her cup and replied, "It is my country that is hurt, my people who are hurting: what else can I do?" It was that sense of solidarity that characterised Haiti in the immediate aftermath of the quake.

Travelling anywhere in the capital to gather information, attend coordination meetings with the United Nations, or meet government officials, was always challenging. During the first few weeks there were not enough cars, or drivers, to keep up with the surge of new personnel and activity. Vehicles that had been ordered sat in heaving warehouses, tied up by a backlog of customs procedures. When a car and fuel could be secured, progress was painstakingly slow as traffic was forced to weave around fallen buildings. Port-au-Prince had been designed for just 80,000 people, and yet, at the time of quake, it was packed with makeshift buildings for 500,000 more. Most of these buildings had substituted sand for the more expensive cement component in the concrete that was designed to hold the bricks together. On 12 January, therefore, they collapsed as easily as sandcastles.

After weeks of these challenges, I was pleased when my team secured a car to visit one of our livelihoods projects, a community canteen in the hills above the city. We made unusually good progress as we climbed out of the capital. Walls were re-adorned with colourful paintings and intricate metal works, fashioned from recycled oil drums. The emerald sea could be glimpsed from the hillside. I felt as though I could almost peek back in time to see the city as it would have been - beautiful, alive and vibrant.

That is when, as we slowed for a particularly steep bend, I saw him.

A delicate young boy, not more than ten years old, was lying face-down on the pavement. People passed by, glancing down and then stepping over and around him. How sad, I thought detachedly, to have died without his parents' comfort and to be lying unnamed and uncollected under the fierce sun. I made no comment to my colleagues in the car and, as the car strained upwards around the next corner, forgot about him.

At the time, it was unremarkable to see a child collapsed, or dead, on the street. Why should it have given me pause? Ten years before, in Srebrenica, Bosnia Herzegovina, I had seen mass graves turn boys and men into waxy, candle-like figures. This boy, on the other hand, lying still amidst the animated crowd, was so immediately a child, a son. Yet, even if I had stopped the car, what could we have done? Surely someone—his mother, a friend—was about to walk around the corner.

What was one more amongst 220,000 dead?

At that moment, I did not think about him as we continued to climb out of the city. I slept poorly again that night, not due to thoughts of that boy, but because of another aftershock catapulting me outside. As more-recently arrived colleagues returned to their beds, bleary-eyed, I realised that I was frozen. I could not find an area safe from the fall-distance of the garden walls, nor could I go back inside, underneath the suffocating weight of the bedroom ceiling. The world itself was inverted as the earth, and my bedroom, usually sources of shelter and comfort, had themselves become the menace. I looked up at the dark sky and thought of my family and the changes in my life. I had never felt so alone.

A gentle squeeze on my arm. "*Ça va?*" Our Haitian security guard was appraising me. His concern unfroze me. "*Ça va*", I whispered and went back inside.

Several months later, I moved to New York with the UN. It took some time to consciously coax myself down Manhattan streets where there was no escape from the shadows of skyscrapers, and to stop jumping every time a subway rattled underneath my feet. As I began to relax, the picture of the boy, lying so alone in the punishing sun, started coming to mind unbidden.

On the anniversary of the quake, I sat in tears in front of a staff counsellor, arms wrapped protectively around my pregnant belly, and spoke for the first time about the child and how he might have become separated from his family. How could I, who become embarrassingly emotionally invested in TV shows about aspiring pop stars and sniffs through Les Miserables, have been unmoved? For it not even to register as a memory until a year later?

Over time I came to understand that sometimes we can be so overwhelmed by suffering on a massive scale that we become numb. Unable to identify individuals within the chaos. Unable to feel, only to see. I came to accept that it was only after I had replenished my own emotional stores that a suppressed memory would be allowed to resurface and be processed.

It was cathartic later that year, during the disaster response to floods that had engulfed major parts of Pakistan, to find that it was possible to regain stores of compassion and resilience. Reassuring to know that our personal earthquakes do not prevent us caring for others again, even if we cannot always respond immediately to each and every little child.

Pakistan
Introduction

Pakistan is the sixth most populous country in the world, with over 190 million people.[1] Located in South Asia, it is bordered by India to the east, China to the north-east, Afghanistan to the north-west and Iran to the south-west, with a long Arabian sea coastline along the southern border. The state became independent in 1947 following the dissolution of colonial British India.

Pakistan's history has been marked by both man-made and natural disasters. While its political, sectarian and terrorist violence continue to make headlines across the world the country has also suffered numerous natural disasters in the last decade.

On 08 October 2005, the northern mountainous region of Pakistan experienced a massive earthquake, measuring 7.6 on the Richter scale.[2] Between 75,000 and 100,000 people died, and at least 130,000 more were injured.[3] The earthquake caused thousands of homes, schools, hospitals, bridges and roads to collapse. Most of the fatalities resulted from crumbling buildings, including thousands of children who were at school that morning.

The remote and mountainous location of the disaster meant that the challenges in providing relief and assistance were enormous. Bridges and roads had been washed away, and thousands of people were stranded, with a bitter winter arriving across the Himalayas.

---

1   "The World Factbook Pakistan"; 11 September 2013. Available from: https://www.cia.gov/library/publications/the-world-factbook/geos/pk.html.
2   "Pakistan: A summary report on Muzaffarabad earthquake"; 07 November 2005. Available from: http://reliefweb.int/report/pakistan/pakistan-summary-report-muzaffarabad-earthquake.
3   "South Asia Earthquake". Available from: http://reliefweb.int/report/india/south-asia-earth-quake-fact-sheet-25-fy-2006; http://articles.baltimoresun.com/2005-10-18/news/0510180139_1_toll-relief-officials-quake; http://www.ijbssnet.com/journals/Vol._2_No._4%3B_March_2011/20.pdf.

Over five billion USD in aid arrived from all over the world, including helicopters, medical teams, tents, and food packages which undoubtedly saved tens of thousands of people from a feared 'second wave of death' as exposure, lack of food, water and illness took its toll.[4]

After the initial emergency period was over, funding was provided to rehabilitate the basic services that had been destroyed in the earthquake. Funds were used to rebuild schools, hospitals and other public services. A major motto of the recovery was, 'build back better', both in terms of improved building codes but also in improved basic services, through the training and equipping of teachers and medical staff. Even before the earthquake, the rates of maternal and neonatal mortality in the area were high as a result of avoidable infections or staff not knowing how to handle a complication.

4   Yauch, Brady. "Banking on disaster"; 23 August 2010. Available from: http://journal.probein-ternational.org/2010/08/23/banking-on-disaster-pakistan-officials-accused-of-diverting-funds-from-earthquake-aid/.

At the Tibetan Reception Centre, where new refugees arriving from Tibet are welcomed, given food, shelter, and clothing, until they get on their feet in Dharamsala, India. ©Jenn Warren

Tsedup, a Tibetan man living in India and former political prisoner in China, covers his face with a photograph of his family standing in front of the Potala Palace in Lhasa, Tibet. ©Jenn Warren

Shattered Illusions
Helen Seeger

It was when the lights went out that I realised it was all going wrong.

Annie and I were in a large district hospital in the mountains of northern Pakistan where the staff managed the delivery of around 500 babies per month. The valley, up towards the border with India in the disputed territory of Kashmir, was devastated in 2005 by a massive earthquake which killed tens of thousands and flattened homes, hospitals and schools. This district hospital was meant to be temporary, built by an NGO in the immediate aftermath of the earthquake, but the pre-fabricated warehouse-like structure remained for several years. At twenty-one, it was my first job in the humanitarian sector, and I was excited to be travelling around in the mountains—to be working 'in the field'.

Annie, an American, was an experienced midwife and a trainer in maternal and newborn health service provision. Grey-haired and twinkly-eyed, she was full of stories and had a tough, fierce demeanor. Our project was a five-year health service and systems project, with ambitious goals around reducing maternal and newborn mortality, improving service quality through comprehensive training and mentoring, and involving the local community in supporting the facilities. This hospital was our main focus—one of nine hospitals and clinics chosen in the area for a major push to increase the number of deliveries in health facilities and the quality of care provided.

As the new Communications Manager for our NGO, I was there to interview patients, take pictures of cute babies and write up a 'success story' or two to send to our donor as part of the quarterly report for which I was responsible. I had never seen a baby born; in fact, I couldn't even remember having been in a hospital before. However, I had grown up in Pakistan, so I hoped I could be helpful to Annie in communicating with the staff and patients.

We went to the hospital for the night shift, arriving at around 4 pm. I'd visited many times but never for a whole shift before. Many men and older children squatted in the parking lot outside, sharing tea and waiting for news from female relatives who hurried back and forth. The hospital was one of the few places in the district which had female doctors and could offer cesarean sections. Many families travelled hours to deliver here even if no complications were expected, fearing the consequences if something were to go wrong in a small clinic far away.

Walking down the dark corridor, we came to the labour and delivery room. Only one of the double doors opened and there were at least seven people trying to go through it in both directions at all times. Squeezing through, we saw that there were already eight women in labour, two to a bed in a small, windowless room. There was barely enough space to walk between the beds as it was so small and crowded. The air was humid, muggy and close. The smell was overwhelming, an earthy fug of blood and feces, laced with a bleachy, sharp hospital smell. I was aware of a low moaning sound, as a woman rocked herself back and forth.

Annie chatted to the midwife on shift, and things seemed relatively calm. We went across the hall to the nursery, where women and babies were in recovery. Annie wanted to check on triplets who had been born the night before. Sadly, one had not made it. Too small, and having trouble breathing, she had slipped away in the night. There was one incubator, in which the remaining two were sleeping next to each other. The mother, pencil thin, was sitting silently with relatives on a bed nearby.

Annie checked on the babies, and looked worried. One of them seemed to have an infection, but Annie was worried about both of them—the sick baby boy, and also the remaining healthy baby girl. The girl was at risk of catching the infection but having been born prematurely, and with only one incubator, there wasn't an alternative. Annie encouraged the mother to breastfeed, and supported her as she got one and then the other baby to feed for a few minutes. The mother was exhausted, slumped on the bed. Annie called the hospital pediatrician, but there was no response. Apparently, the doctor only had morning clinic hours and would not respond to emergency calls at other hours.

Back in the delivery room, at least four of the women were in active labour. I was amazed at how quiet they were. All my ideas about women in labour were from movies and I was pretty sure that there was normally a lot of pacing around, screaming, various medicines, IVs and oxygen masks. I couldn't see so much as an aspirin in this room and these women were toughing it out stoically. The only signs of the serious pain they were experiencing was their wide eyes and the low moaning that sometimes escaped. I wondered whether yelling and screaming were a luxury you get when there's actually a nurse around who can give you an epidural.

Two women climbed up onto the delivery chairs as they were ready to push. The delivery chairs allowed them to sit up in a semi-squatting position or recline partially when they were tired. Annie went in to deliver the babies and I trotted after her. A young woman, who looked about my sister's age, perhaps 17 or 18, was giving birth for the first time. She was terrified, staring at me silently with wide, frantic eyes. I stared back, terrified too and completely unable to think of anything useful to do. I tried to make soothing and encouraging noises, which added a look of confusion to the woman's pained face. I also tried not to look at the rickety old delivery chair, the plastic bucket waiting to catch the placenta or the floor, all of which were marked and stained with blood.

The woman on the next delivery chair had delivered four babies before, and her baby seemed to be coming out really fast. The Pakistani midwife who had been attending to her was in the other room, dealing with a woman on a bed who seemed to be in trouble, so Annie was covering both women at once. It was all getting a bit frantic and hectic, and was making my head spin.

That's when the lights went out. Pitch blackness. The persistent throbbing of the generator died with a sputter, and with no power, the water stopped running as well. The thin trickle of water from the one sink in the corner of the room turned into a drip and then stopped entirely. Without light the commotion and smells seemed to close in and amplify.

I grabbed my phone from my pocket and kept pressing random buttons so that it emitted a small light and Annie could see the head crowning. Annie seemed calm and I could see her feeling in the dark for the tray with the episiotomy scissors that she had laid out. From what she said, I understood that she was trying to decide whether an episiotomy, cutting the skin between the vagina and the anus, would be necessary for this first time mother, while at the same time urging her to keep pushing. I knew that an episiotomy was often better than allowing the skin to tear, but was still worried I might faint, especially as I was holding the only light source.

At the same time, the woman next to us had given birth, but started hemorrhaging immediately afterwards. Annie called for the midwife, and directed her on how to scoop out the blood clots from the vagina and uterus that were causing the bleeding, while attending to the first-time mother and the question of the episiotomy.

Finally, the young woman's baby arrived after a small episiotomy and I couldn't help shouting with relief. The midwife and Annie managed to get the hemorrhaging under control. An hour had gone by when the generator stuttered back to life.

Annie took advantage of the lull between deliveries to go back to the nursery to check on the twins. The situation was worse. Annie tried to call the pediatrician again; again, no answer. We ran around the corridors, trying to find someone to come and attend to the sick twin in the incubator. However, the family decided they'd had enough of the hospital and the doctor's absence, and started to gather their things to leave. They were exhausted, and did not have any hope of the baby's survival. The mother was concerned about her other children, who she'd left with a neighbor.

Frantically Annie tried to explain that the baby needed to stay in the hospital and would die if they left. Seeing that they were determined to go, she asked them to sit for ten minutes, and tried to teach them the kangaroo method of swaddling a baby to the mother's chest, so that the mother acts as a human incubator. This requires round-the-clock care, with different people taking shifts to allow the mother to sleep and bathe.

Ignoring the half-open door and crowd of people just outside, Annie pulled off her own shirt and showed them how to swaddle the baby between the breasts with a length of cloth. She helped the mother do it, and cut a slit in the top of her shirt so the little head could peek out of the neckline slightly. I tried to translate what Annie was telling them—round the clock care, skin to skin, sleep sitting up, you have to be your baby's incubator, someone else will have to take care of the house and the children. But I didn't speak the family's hill language dialect, and I didn't know how much they were understanding. Looking at their tired, uncomprehending faces, I did not have much hope for the tiny baby.

The nightshift ended and the car came to take us back to our office, where we were sleeping in some rooms on the top floor. Back in my room I sat on a chair quietly for a long time, feeling waves of emotion. After the adrenalin of watching the births had worn off I was left with only despair, sadness, anger, frustration, hopelessness. Everything just seemed too broken.

I knew many of the official answers as to why it was broken—lack of budget allocation at the national and provincial levels, poor incentives for female doctors to stay in this remote area, abysmal management, supervision and recognition of health staff, low education and nutritional status of pregnant women—but I couldn't get my heart to understand why, with a multi-million dollar healthcare project, there wasn't more care for those babies, more options for those mothers. I wanted to scream down the phone at someone to send a helicopter for medical evacuation. I wanted to go bang on the pediatrician's door and demand to know what was more important that saving a baby's life. I wanted to steal the incubator and crappy generator and drive up the hill to where the twins and their family lived.

I also had no desire whatsoever to write up a cheery PR piece about donor funds making a difference in women's and babies lives. I could have told the story about the hemorrhage, and how Annie and the midwife had managed it, undoubtedly preventing a woman from bleeding to death. I could have got a nice picture of the new baby all swaddled up and eyes squeezed shut, a quote from the mother saying that she was grateful for the hospital's services and from the midwife saying she appreciated Annie's mentoring and training. But while that is all true, how could that be the story? The real story was much messier, more complicated, bloodier, darker, filled with more despair and hopelessness than anything else.

Years later, this and many other similar experiences have changed my naïve opinion about communications in the development sector. Now, I avoid 'success stories' like the plague. They feel like disingenuous politician spin. I worry that, like politicians' babble, the patronising and simplistic tone and content of these puff pieces undermines the trust of the public and tax-payers whose contributions fund humanitarian work. Perhaps communications are best restricted to factual advocacy on needs and the dire situations of many of our beneficiaries, without the obligatory 'here's an example of how we're making a difference' paragraph at the end.

We all love a story with a happy ending, but often this is a fragile illusion. Perhaps there is a way to describe, explain, and document these stories in an honest and ethical manner, but I don't think I've found it yet. How can we help a tax-payer in London understand and relate to the work we're doing, in a way that shows its importance and urgency but also the messiness and despair? And, on a personal level, how do we fight our own disillusionment at times when the problems seem intractable and the odds against us stacked high to the ceiling?

Syria
Introduction

When the Iraq war began in 2003, Syria could have been described as one of the safest and most stable countries on earth. The same political party had been in leadership for more than thirty years, and the government enjoyed generally widespread support. While Syria was not a wealthy country, Syrians enjoyed benefits such as subsidised fuel and bread.[1] This, combined with strong family networks, ensured that extreme poverty was almost unheard of in Syria.

One of the benchmarks of Syrian national identity, however, was a strong sense of loyalty to fellow Arabs.[2] As one expression of this loyalty, Syria has maintained strong relationships with groups such as Hizbollah and Hamas and has long been on the U.S. list of state sponsors of terrorism and has been subject to a series of economic sanctions led by U.S. Government.[3] However, Syria suffered little from the sanctions because the Syrian government itself was reticent to allow foreign commerce to enter Syria. Coca-Cola, McDonalds and cars less than 30 years old were rarely seen in Syria prior to the Iraq war. The Internet was only introduced in 2000, and mobile communications shortly thereafter; all telecommunications were strictly controlled by the government.[4] This was the status quo in Syria until a U.S.-led military coalition invaded Iraq.

---

1   Irin News. "Syria: Economic reforms threaten social unrest"; 30 October 2007. Available from: http://www.irinnews.org/report/75053/syria-economic-reforms-threaten-social-unrest
2   Seale, Patrick. Asad; 1988. University of California Press, Berkeley. p. 350.
3   U.S. Department of State Website. "U.S. Relations with Syria"; 24 October 2012. Available from: http://www.state.gov/r/pa/ei/bgn/3580.htm.
4   Freedom House. "Freedom on the Net 2012: Syria"; 2012.

Though Saddam Hussein's government fell in 2003, it was not until 2006 that civil war escalated in Iraq, sparked by the bombing of a major religious landmark. During the sectarian fighting that followed, civilians across the country were targeted by various different militias. Some people were attacked because of their religious affiliation, others were targeted because of previous positions they had held in the Iraqi government, and others suffered simply because they were in the wrong place at the wrong time. Life became untenable for many of Iraq's citizens and millions fled to neighbouring countries. Syria was the country that received the largest number of Iraqi refugees: official estimates were that between 2006 and 2009, approximately 1.2 million Iraqis fled to Syria.[5]

Syrians initially welcomed Iraqi refugees, as fellow Arabs, with open arms. Their country served as a safe haven for people fleeing unrest in a neighbouring country. However, an enormous influx of refugees created new problems for a country whose economy had previously been meticulously sheltered from outside influence. Rents began to rise, food prices skyrocketed, and government subsidies decreased. Meanwhile, the international community which had, for the most part, previously ignored Syria, began to take an active interest in the country. International humanitarian agencies set up offices, attracting funding from Western governments to meet the urgent needs of poverty-stricken Iraqi refugees. Journalists began to flock to Syria to document the fall-out of the Iraq war. International

---

5   Marfleet, Philip and Dawn Chatty. "Iraq's refugees – beyond 'tolerance.'"; December 2009. Forced Migration Policy Briefing 4, University of Oxford.

commercial interests saw a changing market and started lobbying to begin trade inside Syria.

As the previously comfortable and peaceful lives of Syrians became disrupted, the country's warm welcome of Iraqis began to chill even though many Iraqi refugees were resettled in other countries around the world where they could become permanent citizens. The enormous economic and political changes happening in Syria during the Iraqi refugee crisis may have something to do with the political unrest in Syria which, starting in 2011, spiralled into a bloody civil war that is currently ongoing. There is now hardly a part of Syria which has not been touched by conflict, and a country which was once considered one of the safest spots on earth has become one of the most dangerous places in the world for civilians.

The scale of the Iraqi refugee crisis in the years following 2006 has been dwarfed by the number of Syrians who have fled to neighbouring countries, many of whom have in fact sought refuge in Iraq, which continues to suffer from ongoing sectarian unrest. In fact, as many as 300,000 Iraqi refugees still remain in Syria because they still feel safer in Syria than they believe they would feel in their home country.[6]

---

6   UNHCR. "2013 UNHCR country operations profile - Syrian Arab Republic"; 15 September 2013. Available from: http://www.unhcr.org/cgi-bin/texis/vtx/page?page=49e486a76&submit=GO.

Shayma Ali, 11, was displaced with her family from Abyan, Yemen due to clashes between Al Qaeda and the government military. Here she attends Al-Jajar School in Aden, Yemen. ©Ansar Rasheed

Children resting after participating in a Water & Sanitation Puppet Theatre raising awareness about hygiene practices in Aden, Yemen. ©Ansar Rasheed.

Of Pastries, Loss, and Pride
Kati Woronka

I blinked through the tears, trying to focus my eyes on the figure in front of me. We stood right outside a bakery and he was handing me a thyme pastry fresh out of the wood-fired oven. The scent of baking bread was irresistible. With a smile he waved the pastry in front of my face, patiently waiting for me to accept.

This man with greying hair and big yellow rubber boots hiked up over his heavy brown overalls was the cleaner at our hostel. He was also a refugee, an Iraqi Chaldean Christian who had fled his home with nothing but his family and his pride. They had left all their earthly possessions behind in Iraq in 2006 and come to Syria. It was now 2008 and little had changed. Syria had opened its borders to Iraqi refugees like him, providing a safe haven and a fresh start, but Syria couldn't protect them from the struggles of starting life anew.

He was the beneficiary not the benefactor. And yet, here he was, feeding me at my lowest hour.

The night before, I'd had a falling-out with our media consultant, a strong-willed woman who was good at her job precisely because she was so tenacious. There had been some miscommunication about sangria and wine, and who was going to buy the cake for a birthday party. I couldn't figure out exactly what caused the confusion, but I was stunned that even after I tried to patch things up, she still seemed to blame me. She wouldn't even concede a half-hearted apology, and nothing is quite as demoralising as an unrequited apology when I didn't know what I was apologising for in the first place.

I forced myself to stay calm and withdrew to my room to work on a report on the status of NGOs in Syria that was about to be overdue. At midnight the phone rang. International call. Inexplicably, before even pressing the little green button, I knew what the call was. But I still forced my mother to say it out loud: my grandmother had passed away.

The report was not delivered to my superiors by 'close of business' as promised and, after the confrontation with my colleague, I was scared to brave the whitewashed hallways of the student residence which was occupied by the team of volunteers I was leading. The thought of running into her was too much to bear. I had never felt so alone.

My grandmother was the great inspiration of my life, a slight, shy woman who had journeyed alone from Poland to the United States in wartime, and who had instilled in her children, and grandchildren, the conviction that our greatest achievements would be acts of sacrifice and service to others. Now she was gone. All my living relatives were in an entirely different hemisphere, and somehow I had to figure out how to travel 6,000 miles to join them. I felt that my teammate had become my sworn enemy, but I still did not know how I'd offended her so much. Nor was I sure whether anyone else on the team sympathised with me, or if they were all on her side. On top of it all, I knew that even though my brain could not put together even a single intelligible thought, I wouldn't be able to relax until I finished that confounded report.

After a sleepless night, I headed into central Damascus with the vague intention of finding a travel agency that could help me get to New York. It was as I trudged up the main street of the expensive and exclusive shopping district, tears welling and threatening to spill, that Abu Girgis found me.

Abu Girgis now supported his family by washing our floors. He had lost his house and more than one family member in bombings during the peak of sectarian fighting in Iraq, where everyone seemed to be someone's target simply because of their ethnic and religious heritage. He and his family were in the first wave of the mass exodus of Iraqis to Syria that began in 2006.

He was a hard worker, short and stout and always on the move, a father of three who had not pursued higher education himself but had supported his brothers in doing so. In Damascus, he had found work cleaning a church in the mornings, then doing housekeeping and helping with the cooking at our hostel in the late afternoons and evenings. He could not make enough money to fully support his wife, in-laws and children, but they were scraping by as they awaited the green light to move to Scandinavia as sponsored refugees.

Iraqi Chaldeans in Syria were proud and classy, and they loved to have fun. I once attended a celebration commemorating the end of a summer camp for Iraqi school-aged children. About 200 kids were bused from their homes in the city's poorer suburbs to a spacious hall in the basement of Damascus' largest cathedral to watch each other perform. The adults sat in the seats of honour at the front, foreigners and dignitaries in the first row so as to be most visible for the cameras. Behind us, the children were arranged tidily by age, circumspectly supervised by youth counsellors who stood in the side aisles. Among the highlights of the event was a fashion show, in which a few dozen primary school children dressed up in different types of garb, ranging from formal-wear to traditional Arab, from ghetto fabulous to karate outfits to a Spiderman costume. There were dance and musical performances and a puppet show. At one point a loud techno beat burst out of the speakers, and a dozen adolescent boys wearing sagging jeans and caps turned sideways hopped onto the stage to show off their break-dance moves.

All the children, both those in the audience and those on the stage, were well-dressed, well-behaved and friendly. The camp counsellors were volunteers, mostly Iraqi teenagers themselves. They did a great job of teaching the kids and keeping them disciplined. They revelled in the diversity of religious and ethnic groups represented by the children in the room - the same diversity which was tearing their country apart. These youth took their jobs seriously, supervising kids during the ceremony then serving cake to us 'important people' afterwards. Once the official events of the evening were over, some members of our team went out for dinner and a hookah with several of the Iraqi volunteers, an evening filled with both laughter and deep conversation.

These people with impressive fashion sense and musical skills, with their ability to have fun and yet still show respect for each other —this was not the image of refugees I'd brought with me to Syria. The Iraqis I met in Syria were hospitable and generous, interesting to talk to and interested in different types of people. Higher education degrees abounded. Doctors, lawyers and academics. Artists, musicians and poets. These were the 'beneficiaries'.

In other countries, I felt a terrible divide between expatriates, including myself, and the people we were there to serve. There was always a name for us: Malae in East Timor, Blancs in Haiti, Khawaja in Darfur. I had a friend in Darfur who was so determined to actually get to know her Darfuri neighbours, that every time a kid on the street would call out "Khawaja!" as she walked by, she would reply in her basic Arabic, "I'm not Khawaja! I'm Sara!" After a year invested in correcting the neighbourhood children, they got the hint and started calling her—and every other white woman who walked down their street—"Sara." It was somehow inevitable: to the people we came to serve, we weren't individuals. We were foreign objects. And, no doubt, our hosts figured we felt the same about them. Maybe we did.

Not so with Iraqis. They stood up and looked me in the eyes and told me what they thought. They invited me to lavish meals in their homes, which I have absolutely no idea how they could afford because I knew that they'd used up all their savings during their first few months in Syria. Each member of a household looked for some kind of work, a way to scrape together a few pennies each day. And the family kept close tabs on churches and mosques and other distribution sites so they could get whatever handouts might help them make ends meet. 'Hygiene kits' comprised of cleaning supplies and basic toiletries were particularly popular, as were 'winterisation kits' with blankets and heaters for the winter. But if a family investigated enough, they could usually find some local institution which was procuring just about any type of item imaginable: the key was to get their names on the beneficiary list. Different charities specialised in different types of kits so the shrewd refugee had to be a skilled networker. Many of the Iraqi refugees in Syria had previously enjoyed demanding professional careers, so learning how to navigate the burgeoning aid atmosphere in Damascus was a challenge which they approached with skill, pride and honour.

Nonetheless, no matter how many kits they acquired or beneficiary lists they got onto, it was a meagre existence that they carved out. It is likely that the Iraqi families who invited me to dinner ate nothing but bread and tea for several days so they could show off the famed Iraqi culinary bounty that I experienced in their homes. They did not do it just for me, the guest, but for the sake of their own dignity. They were not refugees, they were my peers, and they were determined that I acknowledge them as such.

And so, when shortly after my arrival in Damascus, Abu Girgis the cleaner sat down in the hostel lounge and struck up a conversation with me, I found it odd but soon came to enjoy our chats. He told me about his sister in Scandinavia who had sponsored the application for his family to be permanently resettled there. He explained that they had been accepted and were just awaiting the official stamp of approval, a mere formality. But he had no idea how many months, or years, that might take. Then he showered me with idyllic memories of a spacious home in a breezy village in northern Iraq. He asked me about my love interests and I confided in him about my latest crush, who just so happened to share his baptismal name. He became my uncle during my posting in Syria.

Still, his life was crap and I knew it. I knew Abu Girgis worked fourteen hours a day and fretted at night because, with each year of refugee limbo that they spent in Syria, his children fell another year behind in school. I knew that, his show of confidence aside, there was no guarantee the Scandinavian visa was going to come through. I also had but a vague understanding of the trauma he had left behind in Iraq, the awful things he'd seen as his village was overtaken by bombings, both targeted and random, and by sniper bullets snapping throughout each long night.

When I eventually worked up the courage to ask him if he might consider returning home, he said no. Because, "Iraq is lost." I heard this from many of the Iraqis I met in Damascus. One friend of mine told me that if Iraq could go back to what it was before, she'd be the first person on the bus home. But that was not going to happen, not for a long time. If it happened this year, she'd go. But she was sure that it would not, so she and her family were fighting to get resettled in the United States. As I got to know Abu Girgis I became convinced that, while Iraq may feel lost to him already, the loss would actually become permanent when families like his were finally given the opportunity to move on. As soon as the visa came, he and his family would be able to start living again, but Iraq would then truly be lost.

Until the visa came, he was stuck trying to figure out how to survive. Damascus may have been a beautiful and hospitable city, but it was too crowded to suddenly make room for a million Iraqi refugees and there were very few jobs available that paid a living wage. I knew Abu Girgis worked hard but that he still could not afford to buy me a thyme pastry from a bakery in this elite shopping district. I also knew that he had every right to scoff at the passing of my grandmother, who was well into her eighties and ready to move on, in the light of his many personal losses.

But when he asked me why I was crying, I couldn't bring myself to admit that I'd had a falling out with a colleague. And it felt insanely petty to mention my overdue report. So I told him that my grandmother had died.

His response was to buy me a pastry. And then, he put his arm around my shoulder and walked me to a park bench where we sat, side by side, chatting for a few minutes until he got me to break a smile. Then he said he had to go and hurried back to the cathedral where the floors needed scrubbing.

Uganda
Introduction

Dubbed the "Pearl of Africa" by Winston Churchill, the Republic of Uganda is located in East Africa. Landlocked and straddling the equator, it shares borders with South Sudan, Kenya, Tanzania, Rwanda, and the Democratic Republic of Congo (DRC).

From 1987, northern Uganda experienced a brutal civil war between the Lord's Resistance Army (LRA), headed by Joseph Kony, and the Ugandan government. The origins of the conflict lay in the political divide between the north and south of Uganda. The LRA became notorious for large-scale killings and mutilations of civilians of the region, the Acholi people, and for forcible recruitment for its army. An estimated twenty thousand children have been abducted into the LRA.[1] The Acholi people were displaced into camps for internally displaced persons (IDPs) by the Ugandan government's military, ostensibly for their own protection.

Multiple attempts at ending the conflict, peace-talks and military interventions, have occurred over the years, including the Juba peace talks in 2006, which led to a signing of a Cessation of Hostilities Agreement and withdrawal of the LRA from northern Uganda. In response to Kony's refusal to sign a final peace agreement at these negotiations, military forces from the Ugandan government, the United Nations, the governments of Sudan and the Democratic Republic of Congo, supported by the U.S. government, launched Operation Lightning Thunder, in 2008. This failed to neutralise the LRA and now the conflict is regionalised, with the LRA operating

1   "Uganda violence"; 1 Jan, 2011.Thomas Reuters Foundation. Available from http://www.trust.org/spotlight/Uganda-violence.

mainly in the Central African Republic and the Democratic
Republic of Congo.[2]

With the absence of the LRA, security in northern Uganda has
improved markedly since 2007. People have returned from the
camps to their homes and are in the process of rebuilding. But
recovery from decades of conflict takes time, and the region still
faces numerous difficulties.[3] Generating a livelihood is difficult,
with the average weekly income being USD $3.50. It also remains
difficult to meet basic needs of food, agriculture and healthcare.
In the midst of poverty, land disputes, theft and domestic violence
are rife. The population is still seeking ways of ensuring sustainable
peace, which requires discovering ways to promote reconciliation
and justice, making reparation to victims, and ways to document
the atrocities that took place, such that they are not forgotten.

In the far south of the country, bordering Rwanda and the DRC,
the country regularly hosts refugees fleeing conflict in other states.
These numbers rise and fall as conflict waxes and wanes in other
countries. UNHCR estimates that there are 190,000 refugees in
Uganda currently.[4]

2   "No end to LRA killings and abductions"; 23 May 2011; Human Rights Watch. Available from
http://www.hrw.org/news/2011/05/23/no-end-lra-killings-and-abductions [Accessed on 13 September
2013].
3   Pham, P. & Vinck, P.; "Transitioning to peace: A population-based survey on attitudes about
social reconstruction and justice in northern Uganda". 2010; Human Rights Centre. University of
California, Berkeley. Available from http://www.peacebuildingdata.org/sites/m/pdf/Uganda_2010_
Transitioning_to_Peace.pdf.
4   "2013 UNHCR Country Operations Profile – Uganda"; UNHCR. Available from http://www.
unhcr.org/pages/49e483c06.html. [Accessed on 20 October 2013].

Children line up for primary school attendance call in Kyanyawara, Uganda, an area frequently attacked by LRA rebels near the border of the Democratic Republic of Congo. The Kasiisi/Kyanyawara School Building Project, sponsored by the NGO, Cultural Survival, supports rebuilding efforts for local schools in the district, as well as the children's books and uniforms.
©*Jenn Warren*

Kamuzu Central Hospital women's overflow ward, Lilongwe, Malawi, June 2008 ©Caryl Feldacker

Holding Their Stories
Ruth Townley

We are hurtling down a claustrophobic dirt road, heavily overhung by wet season grasses. Despite regulations, our seatbelts are undone. My driver tells me over and over that the precious seconds it takes to unbuckle can make the difference between life and death. If we are attacked, it might be the difference between being inside or outside the vehicle when it explodes. For the occupants of the rusting remains of a vehicle from our NGO that lies nearby, it might have meant getting out before the rocket-propelled grenade hit. The Toyota Hilux jolts in the ruts. First the driver, then I, notice movement ahead.

Silence lodges in my throat like an apricot stone nearly swallowed. There are shapes perched in the trees. I can see their Kalashnikovs. My skin is crawling, awaiting the assault of bullets. Then, we are past the silhouetted danger. Unshot, we crack jokes like sea foam after a wave has broken. Jokes about anything but ambush. There is a slippery film, between the here and now and the nearly was, like an indentation where a forefinger pressed and retracted.

It is northern Uganda, 2006, and such is my trip to work. At the end of the journey, we hurtle into a camp for internally displaced people, bounce over the ditch and settle under a tamarind tree. The air bakes, a mantle settling on me as I climb stiffly down to be met by some of the participants in my group. As with all inhabitants of such a camp, the civil war between the Lord's Resistance Army and the Ugandan government has displaced them from their villages into these sprawling encampments. The remnants of their villages are scattered through the savannah, little burnt testimonies to terror.

Many of the hands in front of me shake, both from the war and the locally brewed alcohol. Some of the eyes won't meet mine. Others stare in what may, or may not, be hostility. Most are smiling. A boy, incongruously, wears a t-shirt that reads 'World's Greatest Mom'. A young woman wears what appears to be a satin nightgown. At the front of the group is a young man, thin, his smile earnest. He greets me with a handshake that is dry and hard, his left hand clasping his right forearm in respect. He is the spokesperson, the informal translator. After lengthy and courteous greetings, he leads me away towards the school classroom we have access to today.

The camp is cankerous and crowded. Cracked earth supports mud huts with thatched roofs nearly touching. A nearby cluster of huts lack thatch and are roofed instead with tarpaulin. A spilt cooking fire, tended by a child, spread through that area recently with devastating swiftness. All around me is the hot stench of too few latrines for too many people and the smell of alcohol brewing. The IDPs here run and hide each evening in fear of rebel attack. They anger the NGOs by eating the seeds they are given to plant. "'We could well be dead by morning, so we may as well eat tonight," I am told.

As we move through the camp, the expectancy of the people crowding around me is nearly unbearable. They want an end to war and I anger them with the sheer inadequacy of my presence. Their neediness is overwhelming, rendering them almost inhuman to me. Sapped by brutality and trapped in this camp, they are victims of war. Unable to sustain life for themselves, NGOs provide them with food, medicine, clothing.

I work for an international NGO. As part of my role, I have developed a programme called Signs of Hope. It involves storytelling and drama. I am here today to run the programme with a group of youth. But it strikes me, moving through the camp, as absurd. Who am I, pink and fed, to stand in front of them and believe in hope? My presence almost shames me. I struggle with myself to come back, to simply focus on the individuals in front of me.

In a long, low building, with its potholed floor, bullet-scarred walls, and dust swept thickly away with short brooms of long dried grasses, a large group is waiting for me. The school room's rickety wooden desks have been dragged to the edges, creating a performance space in the middle. At the desks and on grass mats, the youth are seated. They range from about twelve to twenty-five years old, although, given inadequate nutrition, it's hard to guess at ages. Most have shaved heads. Hair is a luxury where water is a precious resource, queued for, pumped and carried. Ringworms adorn many of the heads. Looking around the group, it occurs to me that all I know how to do is sit and talk. I never feel certain that I bring a worthwhile offering. When water and food cannot be taken for granted, is listening to a story of any value at all? Most NGOs pay participants an allowance for attending a workshop and I have had bitter struggles with camp inhabitants over my refusal to do the same. The measure of success today is that about forty young people have turned up, accepting that I will not pay them to be here. They are here, it seems, for the sake of stories.

The translator introduces me. There is a settling down and warming up process, with translating efforts that require everyone's involvement. I use the small, humbling amount of local language that I possess, intending to thank the translator. Instead, I confidently announce that I am a rabbit. When we are ready, the participants break into small groups.

Each participant is invited to tell his or her small group a story. After a break, the group chooses one story, or a mixture of several stories, to tell to, or act out, for the entire group. They choose their own topics. If I am certain of anything, it is that you don't force traumatised people to talk. If we talk, it is about other things, and if they proffer their stories of suffering, so be it.

As the small groups, one by one, get up to present, they acknowledge me as the facilitator. Although they perform for everybody, I sense that their focus, in some way, is on me. I feel like they are holding something out to me, fragile and tender, easily dropped or lost, as easily deprived of oxygen as the youth themselves. Their stories come to me as images with an aftermath of sound. It is like there is a delay between what I witness and what I understand. It is not disbelief that slows my comprehension. It is horror. These things have happened to these children.

There's a helicopter gunship. It's low and pulsing, savannah flailing beneath it. It follows the children and picks them, sometimes one by one, sometimes in little clumps, expendable little lumps of flesh, involuntarily in the thick of things. The bony-armed boy playing the gunship ack ack acks and rat tat tats his way around the classroom. The others in the group try to run away but fall before him. At the end, they stand nervously, momentarily overwhelmed, and we clap them back to their seats.

The next group tells, rather than acts, their story. Their bodies form a tableau of shame. There is a child hanging head down from a tree, little head with eyes trying to see it all. An LRA soldier with empty eyes oversees the torture, trademark dreadlocks, Kalashnikov cradled. He wears a stolen NGO t-shirt. There is a curling body memory of hopeless horror, of surrounding the hanging child, of watching blood rushing into that little head, of the memory of the taste of those bite by bite moments. Until, eventually, there was silence alone reverberating among the trees. Nausea and guilt, and a girl says, "That's why I didn't run away from the rebels for eight years. I didn't want to be eaten too." There is a head-down silence, and we clap them back to their seats too.

This war is a horror that pulls at my mouth. The children who have returned from this will always have eyes that speak of this. The weeks, the months and years of this. Many do not return. It is not in the nature of vanished children to return. And it is the forfeit and fate of mothers to stay at home, awaiting and mourning the vanished ones, the thousands of abducted children whose bitter adventures leave footprints in blood and fear along the forest floors as they run. I sit here, among these who have returned, on grass matting on the dusty concrete floor. I sit amongst these eyes and struggle to listen. Surely, I think, surely the skeleton that holds me upright can contain so much anguish and hold me upright still.

I struggle to listen and my eyes drift beyond the door of the classroom, where time is still moving. I see mats spread with drying sorghum, hopeful chickens pushed away. Girls with babies strapped to their backs walk jerkily by, a 25 litre jerry can of water in each hand. Women with bundles of firewood on their head walk from the savannah back into camp, one hand up to steady the load, long skirts twining about graceful legs in the breeze. Long horned cattle are driven along the road.

From where I sit, my eyes are met by those of an old man. His torn shirt hangs loosely over the cave of his chest. He is sitting and listening to the stories while he holds a sleeping baby. He smiles at me. For a moment, the complexity of what I am attempting drops away and I relax. I feel at peace. It is a strange sensation. I feel comfortable being still. I hear the words from the group again. "My people", they are saying, "will live on." They are saying, "although we live in war now, we will survive. We will return to our villages and build the campfire in the evening again."

The next small group has built an imaginary campfire in the centre of the classroom and has gathered around it, makeshift props in hand. They tell traditional stories and laugh. The mood in the room shifts. The sullen, sour odour of fear dissipates and the taste memory of human flesh recedes. I am astounded at the capacity of these people to move on, to not linger unnecessarily in suffering. Around this campfire of the future, they are gathered, telling stories of long ago. I am a white girl with a privileged glimpse, an invitation to sit and listen to what suddenly feels like a rehearsal of healing.

The final group takes us outside. The elders are there. I'm not sure why. Some kind of dance begins. My translator is seated next to me, unaccountably quiet when I ask him for the meaning. Columns of people are dancing, fierce and proud as they stomp the red earth. I am conscious of the blackness of their skin, the shine of their perspiration. They stand out, tangible in the bleached heat and light. The leader shakes a spear, its tip fashioned from wood. After a while, I realise they are approaching, their eyes upon me. Their intensity is frightening and exhilarating. I hold still and quiet. The spear advances and halts, the tip just protruding through my lips and touching my tongue. I wait. The spear withdraws, the columns wheel about and the dance continues, wild ululations breaking up the dense air. Other people mosey up and join in, laughing, as the dance changes into something fast and joyful. I feel the drums changing the pattern of my heartbeat.

The translator leans in and whispers that it was a traditional test for a visiting stranger. "You did not move", he informs me, "you passed." Unexpected pride pours in and fills me. I have passed a test I hadn't known I was sitting. I am relieved too. This place is always testing me. It's nice that, for once, it's acknowledged. I ask what happens if you fail. "Traditionally," he says, "we would kill you. But don't worry, these days, we would just send you away."

A swirling, eye-stinging wind begins. It presages a wet season storm and I begin the lengthy and courteous farewells. Such, I think, as the driver and I hurtle out of the camp, scattering piglets and chickens, is another day at work. Racing the gathering storm and the threat of ambush back to town, I notice the day's layers of emotion drifting inside me with the sand and dust drifting down from the wind. I'm holding all those stories in there, like my skin holds the layers of sweat and dirt and sunlight. And, perhaps, in there too is a small feeling that just sitting and listening, at least today, could be enough.

Send In The Clown
Miranda Gaanderse

"Why did you cry?" the burly cameraman asks, as he zooms the video camera lens in on my face. Just moments earlier, I saw the creative spark in his eyes as he glimpsed my crumpled, red face and quickly swept his camera toward me to capture the moment. Perfect. I am the crying aid worker. This will certainly be icing on the cake for this scene in his documentary about a young Danish clown travelling through Uganda. The happy clown, the laughing refugee children, and the crying aid worker. My mind races for something intelligent to say while the clown looks on encouragingly, waiting for an answer.

I am not a big crier. It just happens that today is my last day in the refugee settlement, and I am suddenly feeling emotional about leaving. It has been two months of intense highs and lows, and the reality of my imminent departure has slapped me across the face. It is coming to an end—I am leaving this place. I cannot possibly express the depth of feeling I have at this realisation.

***

Two months earlier, I was based at my organisation's headquarters in Geneva. Since I joined, a little over a year ago, I wanted nothing more than to be sent to the field on an emergency mission. Working at headquarters had given me itchy feet. I no longer wanted to sit in Geneva while my organisation deployed staff to the field to respond to the needs of people impacted by crises in Somalia, Mali,

Sudan, and Syria. I was yearning to be where the action was, to do the 'real' work.

When my name was at last placed on the Emergency Response Team roster for deployment within 72 hours to any emergency in the world I could not have been happier. For months, I obsessively checked Al Jazeera and the BBC for any indication of new turmoil that might lead to my deployment. I realise that sounds morbid. But I was not hoping for something bad to happen; rather since something bad was inevitable I was hoping it would come about sooner rather than later. At least, that is what I kept telling my fiancé, who was growing more and more concerned by my obsessive news-consumption habits.

The call finally came. I was being sent to Uganda. Fighting in neighbouring Democratic Republic of Congo between government forces and the M23—a rebel military group based mainly in DRC's North Kivu province—had resulted in thousands of refugees fleeing North Kivu into neighbouring Uganda and Rwanda.

I flew out three days after receiving the call.

Arriving in Kampala, the capital of Uganda, in the early morning, I was shuttled directly from the airport to the office where I received briefings on my assignment, and discovered that I would be based at Rwamwanja Refugee Settlement.

Rwam… what???

While my fellow emergency roster colleagues were jet-setting off to high-profile emergencies elsewhere in the world, where images of camps hosting tens of thousands of refugees were being splashed across the international news—Yida Camp in South Sudan, or Zaatari Camp in Jordan—I was headed to a place that did not even yield Google results. I know because I checked. Few people had heard of it, and even fewer could pronounce it. Including myself.

I soon learned that Rwamwanja was an old refugee settlement in south-western Uganda, formerly home to Rwandan refugees who had fled the country prior to the 1994 genocide, which had then closed in 1994-1995. It was now being re-opened to host the newly-arriving refugees from DRC. I was warned in Kampala that conditions in Rwamwanja were basic. Difficult, they said. The small team of staff there were living in tents, had limited generator-provided electricity, no cooking facilities, and very basic pit latrines and bathing shelters. So, I decided to take what I considered the most reasonable course of action in order to prepare: I went shopping.

At the advice of colleagues, I amassed a full box of canned and pre-packaged food; a gas cooker and cooking utensils; a sleeping mattress; jerry cans, a bucket and a basin; cleaning rags, soap and toilet paper; and of course, some beer and wine. I was travelling by road with no weight restrictions, so why limit myself?

I soon discovered that there was no shortage of space in the SUV for my hoard of supplies nor was there a shortage of mocking stares and incredulous glance—especially from local male colleagues—

as these supplies were loaded into the vehicle. I had messed up already. I was a stereotype. I was the girl from headquarters who was bringing a whole household with her to a refugee settlement. I could read the thoughts on their faces: "She is not going to last." I smiled to myself—I am tougher than they think.

Upon my arrival in Rwamwanja, our team leader greeted me warmly and gave me a quick tour of our simple living and working compound. He showed me the staff sleeping tents; a larger tent without walls for eating, working and for meetings; a pit latrine for staff; and bathing shelters just behind the sleeping tents, which, he informed me, we shared with the police.

Wait. What? Police?

It turned out that our base camp was directly adjacent to the main station of a contingent of the Uganda Police Force. They had been specially deployed to the settlement for security due to tensions with the local community on land allocation. The deployment consisted of 212 men, and as good neighbours, we all shared the same bathing facilities.

That first night, I timidly made my way down to the bathing area, bucket in hand, for my first Rwamwanja bath. It was dark—there were no lights. I was greeted by a group of five men who were naked but for towels around their waists and plastic flip-flops on their feet.

"You are welcome," they said with kind smiles—beers in hand—and ushered me into one of the cubicles, which was roughly constructed of plastic sheeting. The privacy flap fluttered open and closed in the night breeze. I stood in the moonlight, noticing some suspicious-looking stains on the plastic walls. It smelled like urine. I heard the men laughing and chatting on the other side of the thin wall. I began to wonder whether stripping down in the dark next to a group of half-drunk, undressed, male police officers was really such a good idea.

"I forgot something in my tent," I excused myself lamely, and scurried away. "I will try again tomorrow," I muttered to myself, "before dark."

Sleeping also proved a challenge. There were so many noises, so many footsteps. Our base camp was not fenced, and refugees and locals alike wandered through our camp, sometimes casually swinging the machetes or sickles that they used to clear forest and build shelters. What was more, courtesy of our proximity to the Uganda Police Force, the holding cell for violent offenders and other law-breakers in the settlement was a mere few paces from my tent, and detainees were regularly walked through our camp in order to access the latrines. Although our placement next to the police station was intended for our security, the snoring and other non-security related noises in the night did not instill confidence. Neither did the growing collection of empty alcohol sachets and condom wrappers behind my tent.

I soon came up with a solution to my nighttime noise and security grievances. It required a bit of creativity and the realisation that earplugs were my allies. Before sliding into my sleeping bag at night, I would pull in the zippers of my tent door and tape them together to make it more difficult to break in. I would open my Swiss Army Knife and place it at the ready next to my mattress so that I could cut myself out the side of the tent if someone managed to breach my zipper security system. Then, I would insert in my earplugs—which blocked out noises that would otherwise cause me to startle awake—and drift away in blissful ignorance of all activity going on around me... with the exception of early-morning roosters.

As the days passed, I quickly grew accustomed to the living situation and easily fell into a daily rhythm: Wake up to the sound of roosters. Curse the roosters and threaten to turn them into fried chicken. Check e-mail and do other work on my laptop until the battery dies. Slather on sunscreen. Eat breakfast of bread and tea with colleagues. Laugh. Visit the pit latrine before the heat and the flies make it unbearable. Spend the day working—managing the Unaccompanied Minors Shelter (a group home for children without family in the settlement), arranging for shelter construction for people with disabilities, interviewing and organising support for survivors of sexual violence, coordinating borehole drilling and water point construction, arranging to receive refugees by bus convoys from the Reception Centre, and the list goes on... Remember to be tough. Feel overwhelmed but happy. Return to base camp in the evening, hungry. Gorge on Pringles and Oreos from the stash in my tent. Cheer when the generator is turned on.

Type up inputs into the daily situation report. Curse at having to write a daily situation report. Eat a late dinner (sometimes fried chicken). Drink warm beer that a colleague had stashed away in his tent. Laugh. Boil water. Bathe—preferably alone—at the shelters or in my tent. Set up basins, buckets and pots at places in my tent that are known to leak during the nightly rain showers. Say goodnight to my fiancé over the phone, text message, or e-mail. Sleep. Repeat.

I talked to my fiancé on the phone a couple times a week. Usually, I was so exhausted by the end of the day that I struggled to make conversation, but it felt great and reassuring just to hear his voice. We chatted about his work and his research in astrophysics, and it was often difficult to wrap my brain around it—not only because astrophysics is complex, but also because it seemed so foreign to my current circumstances. We chatted about our wedding and honeymoon plans, which were behind schedule, and it was hard to believe that in a few weeks' time I would be in Canada, walking down an aisle in a white dress. We chatted about life in Rwamwanja. I told him about the good things—refugee soccer games, my newfound love of roasted goat, how great my colleagues were. I vented about daily life—broken down Land Cruisers, faulty generators, my leaking tent. I even talked about work—the complications of coordinating convoys, the lack of safe water for refugees to drink, the absence of partners to undertake much-needed projects.

But I knew he was worried, because he could tell I was not sharing the whole story.

I had trouble sharing the tough stuff. The stuff that made me seriously wonder what the heck I was doing here. The stuff that every now and then made me want to give up on humanity. It was just too complicated to convey over a poor quality phone line, in an e-mail, or even worse, a text message. I did try, but when I did, it came out in a mechanical, matter-of-fact way that separated my emotions and me from the situation. I suppose if I had spoken with emotion, I would not have been able to get the words out at all.

There was no time to be emotional. I had to be strong and press forward. That was my approach. My coping mechanism. But despite my best efforts, the tough stuff remained. Lurking. When I think back to it now, the memories and emotions are still fresh in my mind and in my heart.

***

It is my third day in Uganda, and my first day at work in the settlement. I am in a cornfield, watching a group of refugee men digging a grave for a young boy. He was crushed to death the previous day when one of the buses transporting a convoy of refugees drove off the road and overturned. The family came to base camp this morning requesting burial material—a shovel and mat to wrap up the body. Someone invited me along. I did not have the heart to say no.

So, now I stand under the sweltering midday sun, feeling like a useless bystander as I watch the hole they are digging sink deeper and deeper into the earth. Roasted maize materialises and someone passes around a bottle of Fanta. I desperately want a sip, but do not dare to ask for fear of being rude. Instead, I continue to stand awkwardly with the other women wondering if I should really be here. They did not cover this in emergency training.

The woman beside me begins to speak to me, timidly, in Kiswahili. I do not understand. A young man translates for me into French.

"She says that she thought they had come to a safe place, and yet the boy has died anyway. She wonders if he would still be alive if they had stayed in Congo. She wonders if all the danger they faced to come here was for nothing."

My head starts to spin. A man emerges from the cornstalks with a bible tucked under his arm. Another man emerges carrying a small figure rolled up in a mat.

***

It is three weeks into my stay in Rwamwanja, and I am spending the afternoon at base camp catching up on some reporting. My colleagues are across the road having a meeting with government representatives. We have turned on the night generator so that I can plug in my laptop and I am tapping away in our large multi-purpose tent with the sides rolled up, in the centre of the camp. The roar of the generator suddenly sounds different—an uneasy rumble. It is not the generator. I glance to my right and see a group of about thirty Congolese refugees with machetes marching determinedly down the road towards me. Shouting. I know what this was about—a food distribution is two weeks late. They have been complaining to me for days. Shitshitshit. I freeze and immediately regret not having pushed the issue of fencing for our camp. Thinkthinkthink. What do I do? Hide in my tent? Run into the bush? I stand up cautiously. They would not actually hurt me, would they? Maybe we can just talk it out.

My thoughts are interrupted by a small group of uniformed men charging out of the police station. An immediate sense of relief washes over me. But just as quickly, it sours in my mouth and turns into a wave of nausea. I hear a stick whizzing through the air and landing against the flesh of one of the refugees. Again. And again. He yelps in pain as the police officers drag him from the group and beat him to the ground.

***

A couple weeks later, I arrive at the Unaccompanied Minors Shelter to the call of, "Madame Miranda! Madame Miranda!" The boys are calling to me as I climb out of the white Land Cruiser. I consider it a small personal victory that they now call me by name rather than 'Muzungu'. They wrestle and elbow each other in their attempts to steal a peak into the back of the vehicle—just in case we have brought something for them.

I scan around for one boy. Today is the day; we have made all the arrangements—interviews, assessments, home visits. We are taking him to live with his older sister, who just arrived in the settlement.

He is packed and ready to go. A sleeping mat, a tin cup, a bar of soap, a mosquito net and a plastic washbasin—all his worldly possessions, all of which he acquired here—neatly bundled together. He is smaller than the others, and normally hardly ever smiles. But today day all his teeth are proudly on display. He clambers up into the Land Cruiser. His sister lives about 12 kilometres away, so we need to drive—and he grins from ear to ear as we pull away.

The smile does not last. Two hours later, we are driving back to the Unaccompanied Minors Shelter. We did not find his sister. I cannot believe it. My colleague is certain we were in the right place. Neighbours say they heard she met a man and took off. The boy is dazed. My heart breaks for him. We pull in, and the other boys look confused as he slides dejectedly out of the car. He stands there, looking smaller than usual, tears welling up in his eyes. One boy starts to laugh, but promptly receives a punch from another. The boy, head down, begins to walk towards the shelter dragging his bundle behind him. Once there, he curls up into a ball on the cot he shares with two others and dissolves into tears.

***

It is week six for me in Rwamwanja, and I am again at the Unaccompanied Minors Shelter. This time, I am lecturing the boys about the dangers of eating monkey meat—we are in the midst of an Ebola outbreak. Suddenly, there is a commotion at the police outpost nearby. I catch a glimpse of a man sitting on the ground, surrounded by a group of angry refugees. I rush over to see what is going on. I am informed that he beat his wife so severely that he had thought she was dead. He had panicked, packed a bag and tried to run away when neighbours apprehended him and brought him here. I ask where the wife is now, and then quickly see for myself.

She is being dragged across the soccer field towards us by three men. She is stiff as a board, unable to bend her back. She is barely breathing. Her face looks almost inhuman—swollen, lumpy, black and blue. Covered in blood. "The Congolese say that if your husband does not beat you, then he does not love you," one of the police officers tries to explain to me.

The health centre vehicle arrives. The woman is unceremoniously lifted and deposited into the back. The police then signal for her husband to climb into the back with her. I am furious. The man has just nearly killed his wife, and now they were being transported together? I shove myself between the man and the vehicle, telling him in French to back away. He has to wait for the next trip. The police are perturbed—the Health Centre is on the way to the holding cell, and it will save them time this way. I use my 'don't-fuck-with-me' voice. They relent, and she is taken away.

That night, I fall asleep listening to her husband kicking the door of the police holding cell… each kick bringing the memory of her swollen, deformed face to the front of my mind. I wonder if she will survive, and if so, whether she will ever walk again.

***

The days pass, filled with ups and down—good stuff as well as the tough stuff—until it is the last weekend before my departure—a Sunday evening. My colleagues have taken the afternoon off and gone into town in search of good food and beer. It is raining, so I am already in my tent, wrapped in my sleeping bag, having just completed some reporting and preparing to check my personal e-mails when headlights illuminate my tent. They are back. "Special delivery!" a colleague declares as she pops her head into my tent holding out a black plastic bag filled with grilled pork in one hand, and a Castle lager in the other.

I gratefully accept it and crawl back into bed, blissfully devouring the pork as my Gmail loads… slowly… slowly. There is an e-mail from the coordinator of our wedding venue. The wedding is in four weeks. She is finalising our linen order and needs to know what colour napkins we want. I have already told her yellow, but now apparently there are three shades of yellow to choose from: classic maize, sunshine, or goldenrod.

At this moment, I am suddenly and completely overwhelmed as I realise the absurdity of my situation. I am sitting in a tent in a Congolese refugee settlement. I have just finished writing a report on the number of refugee rape cases and infant deaths over the past month. I am now trying to download colour samples for yellow wedding napkins. Something in my heart snaps. My hands tremble and my eyes burn. I do not fucking care what shade of yellow they are. For the first time since arriving in Rwamwanja, I cry. I cry for the dead boy buried in the cornfield. I cry for the hungry man beaten by the police. I cry for the little boy whose hopes of living with family have been shattered. I cry for the woman who will never recover from the wounds inflicted by her husband. The words on the screen become a glowing grey blur as tears stream down my cheeks, and pork grease trickles down my forearm onto my sleeping bag.

***

That was three days ago, and here I am, crying again.

Today is my last day in the settlement and earlier a senior colleague from Kampala called to inform me that a film crew and clown would be arriving to entertain the children. I am responsible for showing them around and answering any questions. Naturally, I have taken them to visit the boys at the Unaccompanied Minors Shelter. The clown, a young Danish girl, entertained them with magic tricks and balloon games. They loved it, and rewarded her with an unprompted song and dance performance, complete with drumming on plastic washbasins. As they started singing and drumming, I started crying.

I am mad at myself for crying. And to be caught, so publicly.

"Why did you cry?" the cameraman repeats.

I try to collect my thoughts and emotions. I have loved the past two months here. If it were not for my upcoming wedding, I would have extended and stayed even longer. Yes, it has been tough, but it has also been real. Raw. Rwamwanja has exposed me to the best aspects of humanity along with the worst—it has not been just tough stuff. I have seen a community come together to support a family that lost a child. I have seen the deep appreciation for food to fill hungry bellies. I have seen the joy of a boy finally reunited with his mother. I have seen the patience and care provided by health workers to the sick and injured. Most of all, I have seen the way refugees who have lost so much find happiness in life and family, work from morning till night to re-build their lives, and remain optimistic about the future. I have experienced the true meaning of teamwork, and the true meaning of generosity. I am not crying about the tough stuff. I am crying because I do not feel finished here. I am crying because I have to leave.

But I do not tell the cameraman that. I simply respond, "I cried because I have never seen them so happy."

The Great North Road
Rachael Hubbard

JOURNAL ENTRY, October 7, 2012: "I have had my first nightmare and I am afraid that the numbness I have built around my heart is going to wear off. My chest is tight; my back hurts and I feel like I cannot breathe deep enough. I dreamt I was stranded in a hospital in Uganda. The hospital, I believe, was Lachor Hospital. That horrible, horrible place we transported women and babies to when there was nothing else we could do. I was going to be raped and abducted in my dream, like many of my patients in Uganda. There was no way to leave. Feeling vulnerable and helpless has to be one of the worst feelings in the entire world. My body feels sick today; today I will write everything I remember about leaving Uganda. I also want to note that I do not believe that I am fucked up or seriously screwed. I think that I am a human being who is capable of experiencing, living and doing the best I can for the developing world. Yes, there are consequences, but some people are more apt than others to do what I plan on doing my whole life. I am going to take weeks and work on a massive, healing cleanse for my body and soul. Someday soon, I'll head right back out to the bush to serve women. Next time I will go better prepared. Next time I will make different mistakes. Next time, I will be brave and have courageous conversations and stand up for my body and what I believe."

The Great North Road is also known as the Cape-to-Cairo Road and it is one of the longest roads in the world. I lived in a mud hut so close to that road that sometimes I was afraid the intoxicated drivers hauling supplies to South Sudan would plow me over in my sleep. The road is mainly dirt and full of potholes so large that during the rainy season you could swim laps in them; needless to say that when it did rain you could easily become stranded on the road for days.

I, along with many other co-workers at the birthing center, despised traveling on that road, so rough that it could easily have passed as a form of torture. We had to travel each week for hours to get into town for supplies, and it was always an experience. I saw many things traveling on that stretch of dirt: sunsets that took my breath away, hundreds of children walking miles home from school, babies dying in my arms. But none of those things can compare to the day I almost died on the Great North Road.

I am not a veteran of the developing world, or midwifery, nor am I a seasoned humanitarian aid worker. I have yet to scratch the surface of healthcare as a midwife, but everyone starts somewhere. My somewhere was when I decided to pursue all of my births and clinical hours internationally as a student midwife. I spent one year bouncing between the Philippines, Trinidad and Tobago, and Uganda. At first my perspective on midwifery in the developing world was naïve and childish. I innocently assumed that I could easily perform my tasks as a student midwife without any emotional or physical consequences. My experience, as a whole, would prove inspiring and solidifying but I quickly learned that I would make many mistakes. I found out that the caliber of work I wanted to do would take a lifetime of commitment. I learned very quickly that, in the end, no matter what I achieved, I would merely be dust in the wind.

My soul bowed to these new ideals; I embraced them and readily marched into the Ugandan bush to 'catch babies'. However, my experience in Uganda was different from the previous countries I worked in, and I often wonder if I failed because I was not strong enough. My initiation into midwifery in Uganda was not for the faint of heart; it was a road that was an endless gauntlet and nearly cost me my life.

My last week in Uganda proved to be a week from hell. It started and ended with a string of bad births and floppy, nearly-dead babies who needed help breathing. Somewhere in the midst of that week, in a state of exhaustion, I carelessly mislaid a dirty needle—a dirty needle that ended up puncturing a hole in my flesh.

"Um, do you know your HIV status?" I heard myself say.

"Positive."

"Great." Lips quiver. This is what we called a, 'bad kind of Africa day.' But they end, like all days do, even the bad ones.

The next morning I got into our Land Rover/ambulance whose shocks had been battered into non-existence, to drive the devil-carved road for medicine I needed for that needle prick. I travelled with a fifteen-year-old, pregnant, rape victim whose blood pressure was so high I could not figure out how she was not seizing and foaming at the mouth.

True to form, our ambulance broke down on the way there. We were stranded on the Great North Road, in the bush without the necessary medication for my needle prick, and a pregnant kid who was scared as hell.

While our driver and I were figuring out what to do next, I was hit with a fever so intense I could barely walk. Even so, we managed to get the car fixed and drive to the hospital. I had to give myself a pep talk about sucking it up, putting on my big girl panties, and getting out of the car to help my patient. That was the only way I made it inside—barely. I then turned and fell on my hands and knees vomiting in front of heaps of Ugandan women who were lined up with their sick children. Their ebony faces registered only wonder—not pity. I crawled into the backseat to go home convinced that my medicine for HIV exposure was the cause of my fever and vomiting.

After some time passed, I felt better and I went back to the hospital for a lab test. I convinced myself that I probably had typhoid again and it wasn't the HIV medicine making me ill.

"You have malaria," the doctor said and looked me squarely in the eyes.

"Oh thank God," I said, relieved that the medication was not the cause.

I returned to our village armed with Coca-Cola, malaria medication and crackers to fight off the parasite filtering through my bloodstream which, in Uganda, is considered no more serious than the flu.

Everyone should have an angel by their side when death comes knocking at their door. My angel's name is Laureli, and I owe my life to her.

Laureli was a volunteer nurse midwife from Vermont who arrived at the clinic only hours before I got sick. I slept through the night under her watchful eye in our shared mud hut plastered with cow dung and dried grass. I was a foolish girl sleeping on death's doorstep. Death can come creeping for you like a lion stalking its unaware prey. It is sometimes expected, or even welcomed, but mostly it is something that we flee from, something that we fear, if we hear it coming. Which I did not.

The next day I woke and everything happened fast. Body crashed fast. During the night, my body had filled with fluid and I turned a shade of bright yellow like I had seen in jaundiced babies.

"Is my liver working?" I wondered to myself. "Is it going to rupture?" The pain in my abdomen said yes.

Digging. I felt people digging into my shrunken veins to pump fluids into me, but no one could get an IV into my dehydrated veins. I felt weighted down by exhaustion, fluid and pain. I couldn't move. I vomited and looked into the blue basin filled with blood.

"Is that OK?" I asked Laureli, and watched her brows knit together in worry. No, it wasn't OK, but neither of us said anything. I managed to squat in the basin; my piss was black as night. I did not even ask if that was OK.

Meanwhile, my hut was filling with Ugandan staff and neighbors; Ugandans view most things in life like a spectator sport and today I was the game.

Soon after the necessary phone calls were made, I was loaded into the back of the Land Rover. Someone dressed me; someone finally found a vein and fluid flowed in. My body weighed a thousand pounds and I was trapped in it. No one would give me anything for the pain for fear it would cause more damage to my liver. Pain. Nasty, dark pain that was more than I could bear.

My mind drifted out to the road. "Am I going to be one of the many deaths on this road?" I wondered while lying in the back seat. Would I be like so many Ugandan women I picked up in labor, many of whom died in childbirth? How many people have died on this road? How many graves mark the roadside that I have traveled miles on? I was not in labor; I was just dying. Would they dig my grave next?

I remember only two things vividly from that drive. Pulling out of the clinic's compound and turning out onto the road I looked up and saw a massive shade tree. I also remember calling my parents to tell them goodbye. Their voices were calm and loving. What do you say to the people you love most in life when you know you are dying?

The pool-sized potholes tossed me back and forth and I curled up on my side like many of the infants I had been catching. Heat radiated from my body and even though my lips were turning black, I could still taste the road's red dirt in my mouth. I kept thinking that maybe death is not the 'worst' thing in the world to experience, as Laureli kept intoning, "Please keep breathing. Please keep breathing."

"Is this it?" I wondered, "Or, is aid work always like this, and I'm merely graduating to the next grade in the school of hard knocks?"

Is this what it meant to serve mankind? Watching children starve, watching babies die, fever, exhaustion, and fighting to breathe? If this was my first year, I could not imagine what the next thirty would bring. I should have been concerned about my HIV status but I forgot everything I'd previously cared about on that journey down that road.

I made it to the tiny hospital to wait for a plane that would take me away. I remember crawling, blind with pain, onto a cot made of wood. It was like metal pounding against my fragile flesh, full of fever. I was given oxygen which made it easier to breathe as fluid kept filling my lungs. We waited. They came. Two gorgeous pilots and a charming doctor met us and we took off from the only tiny bit of tarmac the town had to offer. We went to Nairobi.

The plane landed. A snowy-haired doctor met me at the private hospital. More blood was taken from my veins, every test imaginable performed.

"I am concerned about your lungs," said the man with white hair.

I could barely breathe on my own. Pneumonia attacked my lungs as severely as the parasite that attacked my red blood cells. I was in the ICU for several days and my twenty-three year old body became as feeble someone who has lived a hundred years. Monitors beeped. Bedpans were full.

"Can I have a pen?" I asked. "I want to write a poem about bedpans." The nurse looked at me in disbelief and ignored the request. Damn it. I secretly unhooked my heart monitor so I could crawl into the bathroom. Head swimming. Nurses came charging in to put their prisoner back in bed. Over the course of the week there were times that I couldn't breathe, or walk, or feed myself or talk but slowly the malaria was coaxed from my bloodstream and the pneumonia from my lungs. Some days were restful.

After a week in Kenya, I was flown home. Wheeled between planes, people stared. My mother and father were waiting for me at the gate to take me home to West Virginia. As we sat on top of Shenandoah Mountain together tears streamed down a face that was weary but not defeated.

I will say that my spirit never broke, and I maintained a sense of humor. I never once questioned midwifery or my choice to come to Uganda. I did, however, gain a better understanding of the gravity and danger that life's decisions can hold. I no longer have the same childish views and my intentions as well were transformed. My intentions are still rooted in empowering women and caring for them in childbearing.

Thankful. I am still thankful for that experience and everything the Great North Road taught me. I am thankful to be alive. I am thankful I was not devoured that sunny September morning. The Great North Road, like any road, has much to offer and much to teach. I was a student of that road for a short season of my life, and what I learned was this: the journey is the destination, and all who are willing to surrender and receive the road's ruts, curves and hard lessons will be stronger for it.

Democratic Republic of Congo (DRC)
Introduction

Introduced to the western world in Joseph Conrad's 1899 story "The Heart of Darkness," the Democratic Republic of Congo has struggled to overcome its troubled image ever since.

Subjected to one of the most brutal colonial experiences on the African continent, the DRC, a country the size of Western Europe, was once controlled solely by King Leopold II of Belgium. Under King Leopold's brutal rule, the Congolese were forced to harvest mass quantities of ivory and rubber or risk being whipped, mutilated, or separated from their families. Under the harsh practices of Leopold's agents from 1805 to 1908, scholars estimate that between eight to ten million people died from conflict, disease, famine, or other causes.[1]

Yet, even after King Leopold was convinced by the international community to turn over the Congo to the Belgian government, the Belgians ruled the Congo with an iron fist, implementing policies of up to 120 days of forced labor in copper, gold, and tin mines, allowing the colonists to use corporal punishment against the population.[2]

During the independence movement in 1960, Patrice Lumumba was a well-known figure who is still highly regarded by the Congolese for his inspiring rhetoric and socialist principles. However, Lumumba's tendency towards Soviet cooperation in a Cold War world inevitably led to U.S. and Belgian intervention

---

1   Hochschild, Adam. *King Leopold's Ghost.* Houghton Mifflin, 1999
2   Ibid.

and support for his assassination and the subsequent rise to power of Mobutu Sese Seko in 1965.[3]

The challenges faced by the Congolese population continued under Mobutu, who is notorious as one of the most effective kleptocrats in history.[4] While claiming to embrace nationalism and changing the country's name to Zaire, Mobutu pillaged the state's coffers and exploited its vast natural resources while the general population languished.

Laurent Kabila, who was backed by a hodgepodge of African states, most notably Rwanda, overthrew Mobutu in 1997. Rwanda had repeatedly warned Mobutu of the consequences if he did not address the problem of the Rwandan genocide perpetrator-controlled refugee camps in Eastern Congo. Mobutu did not listen and the Rwandans, under the guise of a minority popular uprising, invaded. Two civil wars spanning seven years followed, leaving five million Congolese dead due to conflict, famine, and disease.[5]

Even though the second war officially ended in 2003 under Joseph Kabila, son of Laurent (who had been assassinated by one of his former child soldiers), war and conflict in the country persists today. Rape is systematically used as a weapon of war, ethnic conflict is rampant, and natural resources are exploited. In September 2013, Foreign Policy magazine named the DRC as the world's second failed state after Somalia. In March 2013, UNDP

---

3   Kalb, Madeliene G. The Congo Cables: The Cold War in Africa- From Eisenhower to Kennedy. New York: Macmillan Publishing Co., Inc., 1982.
4   Examples of other kleptocrats include the Philippines' Marcos and Indonesia's Suharto, among others.
5   Stearns, Jason K. Dancing in the Glory of Monsters. New York: Public Affairs, 2011.

tied the DRC with Niger as being the worst in the world on the human development index, considering factors of life expectancy, education, and income.

The longest-running UN Mission in the world is still ongoing in the DRC and a myriad of humanitarian and development organisations operate within its borders. However, ongoing conflict, debilitated or non-existent infrastructure, lack of stable institutions, rampant corruption, and difficult government counterparts assure that development challenges will persist for years to come.

Mukandanga tries to encourage her 8-month-old baby boy, Muhoza, to drink water after receiving treatment for an infection caused by the village doctor scratching the boy's throat. Mukandanga brought the boy to the NGO-sponsored Kinoni Centre de Sante clinic in Ruhengeri province, Rwanda. ©Jenn Warren

Mothers-to-be Leonille Mukamutesi, 20 years old, and Emima Nyirasafari, 21 years old, waiting to deliver at the NGO-sponsored Kinoni Centre de Sante clinic in Ruhengeri province, Rwanda. ©Jenn Warren

Traditional African game called BAO, has been carved into the ground here, and the pieces are found rocks. Children search for things to pass the time, as school is not allowed in the camps in Burundi. ©Jenn Warren

Answers Found In Harm's Way: From Congo To Afghanistan

Emilie J. Greenhalgh

After spending any significant amount of time in developing countries, chances are that you will be confronted with a situation where you think that this could be it—you could die. Right then, in that minute—the near car crash, the mugging, the riot, the serious tropical disease—they all have you under their control. At other times, when you're not in harm's way, you can be cold and objective about this life you've chosen which is what allows you to do it again. But in those moments, that happen so quickly, like dreams that dissipate in the moment of waking, you realise exactly what it is that you want or who you are—in case you had any question.

I had been in the Democratic Republic of Congo only a year but I was already ready to get out. That 'already' underscored my guilt in leaving. 'Already' underscored every conflict I had within myself about being in that godforsaken place to begin with. It was a place that I both loved and hated, that I had read about voraciously for years before knowing that I would do aid work there. 'Already' meant that I couldn't take the frustration, the pain, and the ever-creeping sense of hopelessness that was around every corner in a country where there were no answers in sight. Just pain and suffering that would. Not. End.

I didn't know what to do. I did not know where to go or what I wanted. Did I feel patient and whole enough to stay and work for The Cause? Did I want to re-gather my strength to try and work in another disaster prone country and another Cause? Or did I want to go back to those oh-so-tempting comforts across the ocean at home? Those types of comforts would elicit a little sigh whenever I thought too much about them. But then I would reluctantly bring myself back to the realities of Congo: no water and no power, stories of rape and mindless brutality, tremendous untapped resource potential but no real functioning government or security.

Without really knowing it, I craved one of those out of control, dangerous moments because maybe it would remind me of what was really important, what was beyond my uncomfortable reality and my day to day frustrations and desires. Like it or not, those out of control moments brought more clarity to me than I imagine any religion could.

And then I got what I was craving. In this particular out of control moment, I was in a plane over the-middle-of-nowhere, DRC, nothing but jungle and snaking brown river below. We were flying in a 16-person UN plane from Kindu, a dusty, isolated town on the Congo River in Maniema Province back to the civilisation and expat party town of Goma in North Kivu. The plane was at full capacity. In fact, since there were two of us trying to fly from the same organisation and not enough room in the plane, we'd had to fight, beg and plead the staff at the airport to let us both on. They finally did. And just as I was congratulating myself for getting out of three-day weekend in Kindu we flew into a thunderstorm.

To be honest, although I had gone through hellish experiences where my adrenaline would shoot me into a dazed sort of autopilot, what I dreaded most was flying. Something about the frequency and banality of flying combined with the gnawing thought that giant pieces of metal really shouldn't be physically able to stay up in the air made me say little prayers while searching for the first round of wine on the drink cart that banged past my elbows. There was no drink cart on the UN flight and you could see into the cockpit. This did not make me feel better.

It also did not help that Congo was pretty much considered the plane crash capital of the world. Most humanitarian organisations took UN and EU flights because of the horrendous safety records of domestic commercial airlines. However, with poor traffic control, terrible weather, and rumors of intoxicated pilots, we all boarded flights grimly, gritting our teeth into little smiles at one another and trying to make small talk. Just the year before, a UN flight had crashed when trying to land in a rainstorm, killing all on board.

On this particular day, when we entered the storm, I had been half asleep, eyes fluttering and iPod blaring. Then, the light changed in the plane. Instantaneously, the sun was extinguished by thick, heavy rain clouds. The sky was sickeningly dark. Rain streamed across the windows sideways and the plane started swooping through the air like a ship tossed on ocean waves. I removed one ear bud; no one spoke. I gripped my chair and that feeling came over me: the frozen, adrenaline-induced feeling made all the more intense enclosed in a small plane. I imagined that our grisly end would take endless minutes instead of the swift resolution of, say, a car crash. So many minutes of fear, so much time to think.

All I could think about was my life up until that point and if I was ready to die that particular day. Ensconced in the numbness I couldn't get away from these questions. I felt like I had already accomplished a lot, but was it enough? How had I even ended up there that day?

I had arrived in Kindu about two weeks earlier on the way to Goma. Normally based in Bukavu, South Kivu, I was given the opportunity to travel to Kindu and Kasongo, the two major towns in Maniema Province for two weeks to gather information on a highly successful agriculture project that was nearing completion. Even though this project had received millions of dollars and had produced great results thus far, it was not well known, not trendy or glamorous or anything that would show up from a charity in your mailbox during the holiday season. We suspected that it was because no one really cared about Maniema Province despite the somewhat ridiculous rumors that during the recent civil wars local militias engaged in cannibalism of Italian mercenaries who were captured. That's where it got its nickname: Maniema—*Le province qui mange les hommes*—the province that eats men.

All eyes were on the Kivus and Oriental Provinces of Congo instead, where armed groups and local militias ran amok, terrorising the population, exploiting the mineral wealth, and carrying out ethnic vendettas that had been going on for as long as anyone could remember. In short: the type of crises that were a humanitarian organisation's dream.

Directly bordering more developed Rwanda, access to the Kivus was easy, funds were readily available, and so they were awash in foreigners who brought a myriad of programmes to match Congo's problems. And yet nothing seemed to work. We all tried not to step on each others' toes too much, but the reality was that when working in rural areas you would inevitably run into at least a few Land Cruisers from other organisations, followed by village children yelling "MONUC"—for *la Mission de l'Organisation des Nations Unies en République démocratique du Congo*—the UN Mission to the Congo (the longest running UN mission in history).

Frustrated with this whole set-up, I often asked myself if there was not something wrong with NGOs competing with each other for money and territory, being followed by villagers with their hands out, who were totally unashamed to ask for money, food, clothes, or whatever they saw you carrying around at the time. Combined with this was the unsettling feeling that we were not necessarily helping the poor and vulnerable in the way that we should. Most programmes were run like we were living in a state of emergency that would just never let up and we were eagerly throwing money at the problem without any tangible benefit. I had felt a strong connection with Congo as my father had worked there in the 1970s and it is where a former long-term boyfriend's mother is from. I had read about the country with such interest and yet, once there, all I found was frustration. The romance had left almost the instant I arrived, quickly replaced with the feeling of futility that we all tried to forget while commiserating at the local expat bars in Bukavu. My disappointment in the scene and in my own lack of ability to persevere for The Cause made me a little bit sick.

So, when asked to go to Maniema, I did not hesitate. I wanted to get away from the crunch—from the highly visible, political Kivus for a place that no one talked about, or had even heard of.

"Make sure you take a book or two. And bug spray, and clothes you don't care about. It might also be a good idea to bring some food, unless you don't mind eating the same thing for lunch and dinner, every single day that you're there," my colleague advised. Perfect. The old romance of the Congo and my Peace Corps days was beckoning.

In order to get to Kindu, I had to fly. I was told that only a decade or two previously, it had been possible to drive from Bukavu. However, the road had fallen into disrepair and was eventually swallowed up by the forest, the mud, and the torrential rains. What had previously been a two-day drive now was completely impassible and any cars in Kindu had to be flown in by plane. That's right, cars flown in by plane. The feeling of isolation and inaccessibility was palpable upon arrival. It was little wonder that hardly any organisations operated there.

Kindu itself was a mess of a city on the Congo River: horribly humid, dusty, with unfriendly locals who catcalled as I walked down the road. I found the town overwhelming and was grateful when I discovered a quiet riverside bar that served warm beers which had been flown in and cost five times as much as in Bukavu. As the sun set and I walked home I felt, within the darkness and remoteness, a deep sensation of calm returning to my nervous system. The questions were at bay. I breathed a little sigh of relief, not completely unlike my sighs when longing for the comforts of home far away.

We stayed with the priests at *"la procure,"* a kind of Catholic guest house for visiting priests and foreigners who did not want to take their chances in a local hotel. Our pocket-sized rooms did not have bathrooms and the only lights were small and powered by solar panels. The foam mattress was about two inches thick, and had neither pillow nor blanket. I discovered that I did not need either as the humidity and lack of air in the room meant that I was constantly sweating while trying to avoid the edges of the bed where the mosquito net was tucked in, keeping the swarms of mosquitoes at bay. I felt blessed to have a little enclave where I could give myself a cold bucket bath. It was so hot and dusty I looked forward to the cold baths each evening. I wrapped myself in this ascetic lifestyle for the first few days, reveling in the simplicity. But in the back of my mind the questions were starting to peek out of their locked box.

Every day during my week in Kindu, I climbed on the back of a motorcycle driven by one of our Congolese colleagues to travel for an hour or two over washboard dirt roads that sometimes were no more than a tract through elephant grass, to talk to project participants. Every day I would get back to Kindu and my French colleague and I would go to the World Food Program offices and warehouse, to 'borrow' their internet connection. Our office did not have internet—something someone in our main office in the capital city had overlooked at one point and never remedied. The

WFP guys tolerated our presence, using it as a chance to gossip and flirt, catching up on the non-existent expat happenings in Kindu.

Three days into my stay, I got an email from a former supervisor, explaining that she may have a job for me, somewhere in Asia. The question box in the back of my mind burst open even as I tried to tell myself that this ascetic life was the panacea I would need to fall back in love with the Congo and restore my faith in my work. I expected this little stint to kick-start my motivation and remind me of why I had chosen this ridiculous, romanticised, ideals-driven life in the first place.

And yet, images of Asia flooded my mind. I had only discovered parts of it—India, Hong Kong, Thailand, Laos, Vietnam—and I wanted more. There was something that had hooked me while I was there and it made me giddy just thinking about going back. These were not unlike the feelings I had after I studied abroad in Senegal—total fascination, total excitement about the prospect of going back to Africa. Maybe it was just the idea of going somewhere else that grabbed me. Even though I was loathe to admit it, anywhere seemed better than Congo. "Quick fix," whispered the question box, which was now leaking self-criticism which had, until then, been buried somewhere near the bottom.

Then, right in the WFP office, right at the end of the workday when everyone was about to pack up and leave, one of the elusive directors of my organisation called me. Needless to say, I was totally unprepared for what he said next.

"Well, Emilie, the way I see it, there are three positions that could be available to you right now. The first one is in Bangladesh. The second is in East Timor. With both you'd be alone in remote office most of the time. That's not what you want, is it? So, that's why I want to talk to you today about coming to Afghanistan."

Silence.

I expected to have some sort of visceral, negative reaction. But instead, I was intrigued. There it was, the chance for a new disaster, a new hopeless case, a new fix to grab my motivation and reinvigorate my patience. "I'm listening," I said.

But, in truth, I was hardly listening. While he went on about the nice city where I would be located, the beautiful gardens, the amazing work, the good food, the fantastic colleagues, I was transported to Afghanistan. I somehow knew that Afghanistan was it; that I would be going there next.

A day later, my French colleague and I were on a small, flat-bottomed boat crossing the Congo River, then piling into the back of a Land Cruiser full of food stuffs, engine oil, and several nuns bound for Kasongo. It was a 7-hour drive, riding sideways on the benches in the Land Cruiser, hot as hell and completely uncomfortable. Afghanistan and the questions were pushed to the back of my mind as I stared out the windows at giant trees punctuated by solitary villages. They seemed to have existed there for centuries and would exist for centuries more without any contact with the outside world.

We drove and drove on an unpaved road through the jungle, the dense, huge trees creeping up on either side, not allowing us to see in more than a foot or two. As the day progressed, the landscape changed and elephant grass savannah replaced trees. The grasses towered higher than the car. Every once and awhile, we would pass more villages composed of mud huts, some with solar panels out front. There were no cars, no TVs, hardly any cell phones, and no infrastructure for electricity or running water. It was becoming very clear to me that I was in one of the poorest places I'd ever been and, again, the ridiculous romance grabbed my ankles. Why would I want to leave this fascinating place, this place where I had concentrated so much interest and energy, to go to another?

Every day I went to see some new project, driving in the Land Cruiser over footpaths, not roads, like it was nothing unusual. One day, we arrived in a village where they had prepared chicken and rice for us—a very costly endeavor for people who had next to nothing. The chief informed me that this was a custom they upheld, once common in many places in Congo but that had fallen by the wayside. He also asked me not to forget the people of Maniema—who appeared to be left alone in poverty due to the region's relative peace. Hardly any NGOs worked there. Access, was one thing. It was a logistical nightmare and internet access was prohibitively expensive and patchy. Without electricity or water no expat would volunteer to live there, where UN planes hardly ever landed because of a lack of passengers. Apart from missionaries and Lebanese money lenders there were no other foreigners and there was nothing to do.

The questions came again, nagging at me even in the quiet solitude of this place. This was the type of location the idealist in me wanted. This was the iconic work and the seemingly untainted connection with local people that brought me back to my initial reasons for wanting to live overseas in developing countries to begin with. And yet, I didn't want to live there. For all of the romance, for all of the life lessons I would learn working there and all of the selfless sacrifice I would make doing work that might actually make a difference, I couldn't do it.

I marveled at the kindness of the villagers, the effectiveness of the project, the determination of the staff and heard their plea to bring more resources to help the people of Maniema. But, after two years in Peace Corps giving up everything I wanted I was not ready to do it again. Even knowing that I couldn't live in a place like Bukavu without feeling frustrated and restless, I was too selfish to stay in Maniema or any place like it. I wanted those sigh-worthy creature comforts and connections with other foreigners who knew what I was going through. I knew that this was where the work really needed to be done yet I could not sacrifice my desired ideal life for it.

"But would I really have everything I needed in Afghanistan?" I thought. "I must be crazy to even consider going there after living in Congo."

After making the seven hour drive back from Kasongo I was eager to leave Kindu. The three-day weekend was coming up and I could not bear the thought of being stuck in my tiny, airless room with nothing to do, so there I was at the airport, dreading the flight but begging to be let on the plane back to the place which frustrated me so much. I wanted to go back to the social expat hub to see my friends and eat a meal that did not consist of rice and pounded cassava leaves. Two weeks away and I was ready to forgo my lofty ideals for a few drinks and a few laughs with people I could easily relate to.

And then we flew into the thunderstorm, and I started to again question what exactly it was that I was doing.

Again, I thought about what I had accomplished: college, Peace Corps, graduate school, humanitarian work. It was pretty textbook, following a path that would give pretty serious bragging rights at high school reunions. I regretted that I had never been married or even been in a serious relationship that seemed like it could turn into marriage. I regretted being so stubborn about adopting this lifestyle when I was my mother's only child. But mostly, I was angry that I had not been able to find a balance between the fascination of the crisis, the romance of the humanitarian work, and the blatant desire of a twenty-something woman to have fun and not to simply revel in chasing the misery the world dishes out every goddamn day.

And with that anger I knew I had to get out of Congo. I couldn't find the answers to my questions in teeming Bukavu or in isolated Maniema, but maybe I could find them in Afghanistan, in the new romance, in the new, distorted fun that could present itself in a new crisis.

That is when I realised, despite the possibility that I would die without having had a family, that I did not want to die without going to Afghanistan and putting myself through a different kind of hell. I did not want to leave so many of my questions unanswered. I was just getting started. If I could get out of this, I vowed that I would go to Afghanistan and, that from here on out, I would call my mother before I got on a plane to remind her that I loved her.

Then, the plane stopped bucking and we exited the storm. Somehow, still in one piece.

Finally, when we landed, the entire plane remained silent. The pilot poked his head out of the cockpit and said, "Well, we're here. That was interesting." None of us replied. We just got off the plane and onto the bus.

"*Ca, c'etait pas bon*!—That was not good!" Someone eventually exclaimed. Others on the bus erupted in agreement and grumbling. We were safe on the ground.

And I was going to Afghanistan.

Nigeria - Niger Delta
Introduction

Located in West Africa, Nigeria is bordered Benin, Chad, Cameroon, Niger and the Atlantic Ocean. It is the country with the highest population in Africa and its economy is second largest in Africa.[1] Approximately half of Nigeria's population is Christian and half are Muslim creating tensions in some regions.

The country is named after the Niger River which runs through the country and into river's delta region which also hosts a large oil industry. The country's economy is heavily dependent on petroleum and oil industries with 70 percent of its budget coming from oil revenues.[2] The Niger Delta is an area of approximately 70,000 square km and comprised of nine Nigerian states.[3] Environmental issues related to oil exploitation are a major concern for the Niger Delta.

In the early 1990's tensions grew between the government, the foreign oil corporations they support, and a number of minority ethnic groups in the delta region where approximately 23 percent of Nigeria's population live. Frustrated by environmental degradation and a lack of wealth-sharing some groups took up arms against the government and oil companies which resulted in violent attacks and kidnappings throughout the 1990's. The government responses to the insurgencies were heavy-handed resulting in further conflict and the splintering of rebel groups which had varying alliances with each other.

---

1   Wikipedia. "Nigeria". Available from: http://en.wikipedia.org/wiki/Nigeria.
2   Revenue Watch. "Nigeria". Available from: http://www.revenuewatch.org/countries/africa/nigeria/overview.
3   Wikipedia. "Niger Delta". Available from: http://en.wikipedia.org/wiki/Niger_Delta.

In 2009, the government announced an amnesty and pardon to the rebel groups and some rehabilitation programmes were enacted. While this has decreased violence in some areas, fighting still continues in others with an estimated 1,000 people still dying each year as a result.[4]

Human rights and advocacy groups in Western countries have been vocal about the environmental and human rights abuses in the region.

---

4   Shah, Anup. "Nigeria and Oil"; 10 June 2010. Available from: http://www.globalissues.org/article/86/nigeria-and-oil.

Memories of the Niger Delta
Wendy Bruere

Conversations about the Niger Delta, an oil rich area in southern Nigeria, always seemed to touch on kidnapping in one way or another. It was late 2011, and things had settled down from the 2008 peak when kidnapping of oil workers was a near daily occurrence. But, it was still a hot topic and a real risk for anyone with fair skin or money.

Kidnapping had emerged in the Delta as part of militant opposition to oil companies that were causing catastrophic pollution, but it also proved an effective business model. Criminal groups—sometimes comprised of former militants—began to use it purely for financial gain. But the lines between political and criminal kidnapping were often blurred and, for an outsider, it was sometimes hard to tell where one ended and the other began.

I was based in Senegal and headed to the Delta to spend just over a week gathering information on humanitarian and human rights issues. And, frankly, I was a bit anxious. I was also excited. I'd been interested in the region for over 10 years, since reading about Ken Saro-Wiwa, a peaceful environmental activist from Ogoniland in the Niger Delta, who stood up to the Shell company and was arrested, then executed by the military regime after a widely condemned trial in 1995. Sixteen years on, oil companies continued to pollute on such a massive scale that a 2011 United Nation Environment Program report described Ogoniland as so severely contaminated that a clean up would take decades and cost over one billion USD. Activists working in the area told me this actually understated the damage and impacts, and complained the report covered only a tiny part of the polluted region.

The peaceful protest movement still existed—some of Saro-Wiwa's surviving colleagues remained active in it—but militant groups had now formed and regularly destroyed oil infrastructure and took oil workers hostage. To combat this, the government had developed an amnesty programme where men who handed over their guns were provided with skills training and paid a monthly stipend not to fight.

And—beyond the oil related issues—in the city of Port Harcourt, the state government was threatening to demolish informal settlements along the waterfront where hundreds of thousands of impoverished people lived.

But trying to untangle the facts about Nigeria from outside the country was complicated. The country appeared violent and the politicians I tried to line up interviews with were frequently elusive.

Before I left for Nigeria, I googled kidnappings in the Delta, and tried to work out what the survival rate was. It seemed to be high, so that was good. I also googled HIV rates, and tried to work out what the chances of contracting the disease were in a kidnap-plus-rape situation.

I spent my first full day in the Niger Delta in the oil city of Warri where my fixer—a well-connected local journalist, Abah, whom

I hired to translate, line up meetings, and generally assist—had managed to get me an interview with some former militants. These men had accepted the government amnesty and were currently being trained as welders. Abah and I arrived at a rundown apartment block and were met out the front by the most muscular man I'd ever seen in real life. He was shirtless and holding a knife. He looked like he should have been on TV. He introduced himself as Kempare and took us upstairs, hastily putting down the knife and donning a T-shirt with the slogan 'I'm for Non-Violence' across the front.

The room he took us to was missing doors and windows, and was furnished with a mattress on the floor, plastic chairs and empty beer bottles. Half a dozen other young men strolled in and out to see what was going on.

Kempare seemed to have been coached for the interview, and it was hard to get any real information out of him. He wanted to tell me about the training programme he attended, and he listed what materials they needed the government to supply. The next man I spoke to, Jeffrey, was slightly less prepared and gave me some of the details I was looking for. He told me how in his militant days he, "destroyed oil pipes, you know, and we would hijack and kidnap white people to make the government come and listen to us."

Partly due to my own self-interest as well as the research I was there to do, I tried to find out how hostages were treated. Jeffrey was reluctant to discuss the details of his past, however, and there were plenty of awkward pauses as I kept prompting him. "So, um, how long did you keep them hostage for?" I tried. "Did anyone ever get ... hurt?"

Jeffrey seemed offended by the insinuation he might have harmed anyone. He assured me that no one was killed and all his hostages were freed eventually. And, while he agreed there had been ransoms, he insisted that as they were feeding the hostages some money had to be involved. He said he couldn't remember exactly how much.

He also explained why he did it. He had watched the pollution destroy his community's land and water sources. He saw people die after oil companies dredged the river to make way for the tankers, turning the freshwater to saline.

"A desperate man will do anything to survive," he told me, adding that his community had mostly supported him even though by destroying oil infrastructure he had ultimately added to the pollution.

"We thought after we damaged oil pipes the government would come and make peace," Kempare told me.

And that's what the government had promised to do. Part of the amnesty programme was an agreement to improve conditions in the local communities. Jeffrey had taken the amnesty because he said he believed the government would uphold their end of the bargain, but so far, he said, nothing had happened.

I asked Jeffrey if he felt any guilt about what he used to do. I meant the hostage taking, but he only answered in reference to the destruction of oil infrastructure. He told me he knew this had contributed to the pollution that had destroyed his community's environment and livelihoods. And when he put it like that, I saw why scaring some oil workers didn't register as cause for remorse.

I felt reassured after talking to him though. He and his friends seemed like nice enough guys, keen to sort out the issues and free hostages as efficiently as possible.

When I returned to Australia, friends asked if I was scared in that interview, but that was one of the times I was safest—no-one in that room had any reason to hurt me and plenty of reasons not to since they all received payments under the amnesty programme.

That didn't stop me from waking each morning I was in Nigeria running through the risks I might face that day. But not even genuinely tense situations felt dangerous in the moment, including one occasion when my driver picked up an agitated stranger with bloodshot eyes—despite my shouted attempts to veto the new passenger—and they both started demanding extra payment from me.

From Warri, Abah and I took a speedboat through the creeks that criss-crossed the Delta to Oporoza—a village that had been bombed a couple of years previously by Nigerian forces after being identified as a hotbed of opposition to oil extraction. It was the same story there. Young men, frustrated by seeing their land and water polluted, the wealth sucked out of it and nothing given in return, had eventually picked up arms to fight back.

People told me how they wanted schools, universities, development, jobs, but got nothing but the glare of gas flares, poisoned water, and bombs. For decades before they turned to violence, opposition to the oil companies' damaging practices had been peaceful. But even peaceful protest could bring violent retaliation.

Kempare came to Oporoza with us. Initially, I assumed he was just hitching a lift since someone was paying to rent a speedboat, but he stayed with us the whole day and returned with us.

When we arrived we had to wait for half an hour for a village leader to come and show us around. While we waited, Kempare chatted with some other men in the local language. The English word 'kidnapping' was thrown in every second sentence and I wondered at what point I should start to get nervous. I also started to wish I had told someone where I was going that day. This may sound like an elementary mistake, but I wasn't supposed to travel by boat, and I didn't want to be thought irresponsible, so I simply hadn't told anyone what I was doing.

It was only on the way back that Kempare explained he now helped enforce the law: "I catch kidnappers and give them to the federal government."

He did this because he wanted his region to stay calm so his payments from the government under the amnesty programme would continue. I realised he had probably joined us as a sort of freelance vigilante to make sure I didn't get myself into trouble on his turf.

In Oporoza, village leaders took us to the ruins of the palace of the Gbaramatu kingdom which had been bombed in the 2009 assault. The ruins, for some reason, were guarded by ostriches, which our guides kept at bay by whirling lengths of pipe several metres long round their heads as they ushered us past. I could see how grand the palace must have been, but, as I reluctantly trudged up the decrepit stairs, I was mainly just concerned it would collapse around us. I also knew that this was old news—while I wanted to keep the locals happy by showing an interest in what mattered most to them, I needed details of the current situation, not a repeat of what had happened two years previously.

Eventually, their organised tour over, a group of young men and the village chairman, Elekute, sat with me under a tree to talk.

"We are freedom fighters, not militants," the young men told me.

They asked me when something would be done to help them. Other Westerners had come to speak to them before, they said, and they had told their story again and again. So, what was I going to do for them? I tried to explain my role—I would advocate for them, but I had no power.

As we travelled back from Oporoza, Kempare told me: "Now is the time for peace." He seemed to believe it and said he just wanted to work—even if he had to work for the oil companies. He had two children and a wife to support, and he was tired of watching his community live in poverty.

"If I had a job, and if someone in my village didn't have a bed, I could buy them one," he said. But if the government stopped making the amnesty payments the fragile calm, he assured me, would disintegrate.

Meeting former militants like these helped quell my fears about personal safety. But that changed a few days later in Port Harcourt. Some local activists took me to the waterfront settlements— essentially slums—to meet the people whose dwellings would be levelled by planned demolitions. The state government wanted to clean up the area and develop the waterfront real estate.

As we entered the area, a group of young men stopped us, asking questions about who I was and what I was doing. I explained my role as simply as I could. But when I asked if I could take their photograph everything instantly tensed up. The activists hustled me away. And after that they didn't seem to want to take me far into the slums, preferring to finish up quickly and leave. I figured everyone was tired, and so was I, so I didn't push it.

Afterwards my fixer—a new chap called Itoro as Abah had remained in Warri—explained the young guys were part of a criminal gang, involved in drugs and kidnappings, and that they only left me alone because I was doing human rights work.

"What would have happened if I hadn't been doing human rights work?" I asked, sceptical that I could have been close to danger and yet totally oblivious. "I'd have been robbed?"

Itoro was initially reticent to answer but then told me I would have been kidnapped.

Despite knowing the risks and having been through a simulation hostage scenario in a personal security training, that was the moment when I realised just how terrifying it would have been. I had met the guys who could have kidnapped me, shaken their hands, looked at their faces, and seen the shacks where they lived. It lent an uncomfortable level of detail to my mental pictures of what it would be like to be totally at their mercy for an unknown period of time.

I spent the next 24 hours simultaneously high on adrenaline and feeling like I was going to throw up. I attended a meeting of activists on Ken Saro-Wiwa Day—an annual commemoration of his death—and struggled to focus as my stomach clenched every time I thought about the young men in the slums. The adrenaline outlasted the queasiness though.

And I still went back to the slums two days later because I needed more material. I went to a different area that was meant to be safer. But when we arrived and I checked my watch, saying I would need to leave in two hours, my local contacts told me we couldn't stay that long. "We don't want to give people time to plan anything," they explained. I didn't feel unsafe, but I wondered if I should.

Finally, in Nigeria I also visited Bodo, a community in the Niger Delta that had suffered immensely from oil pollution, and saw firsthand the oily film on the river, and the barren mud banks that used to be covered in mangroves. I watched children swim, and listened to people tell me how there were no fish anymore and how the fishermen had to travel for hours to find their catch now. A young woman told me matter-of-factly that her uncle had died due to a respiratory condition caused by toxins pumped into the air by gas flares. Other people told me about the increased rate of miscarriages, skin diseases, and other health concerns, as well as the damage done to the local economy when the water became undrinkable and the soil unable to produce crops.

In only a week in the Niger Delta, activists, locals and ex-militants put vast amounts of time and effort into showing me what was happening, and helping me find information. While politicians and oil company high ups—who officially and unconvincingly insisted that they were in the right, that no-one would be left homeless by slum demolitions, that they had cleaned up the oil spills in Bodo—were impossible to pin down, only agreeing to short phone conversations after I had left the country.

The frustration I felt was obviously nothing compared to that felt by the people whose lives were destroyed by pollution, or who lived in fear of having their homes demolished. And I admired the quiet patience of these people, who with no guarantee that anything they told me would make any difference, were still prepared to keep trying to get someone to listen to their stories—most of them still hoping that despite all they had experienced, a peaceful solution could be found.

A few weeks after returning to Senegal my contract ended and I went home to Australia still pumped up with adrenaline, though concerned about my ability to judge danger. My head could tell me something was a bad idea, but my heart—in the moment—always seemed to think it'd be just fine. Back in Melbourne, I wondered whether I should chase down the next adventure or whether I was being breathtakingly irresponsible and should stay put.

I suspected if I was a man I would be confident I'd be considered 'brave', but, as a woman, my instinct was to be cagey about what I'd done so people wouldn't think I was foolish or asking for trouble.

The next job I was offered was in Jordan, however, and was perfectly safe. So I took up rock-climbing instead, wondering if that might be a better way to chase the adrenaline high. A year and half later I ended up in Iraqi Kurdistan, still in a stable region, and was contacted by my previous employer to see if while I was in Iraq I would be interested in doing some research in more dangerous parts of the country.

Instead of jumping at the chance, as I would have earlier, I said I didn't know the country well enough to be able to safely take on the task. It wasn't until after I sent the email that I realised I was probably now making better security judgements than I had in a long time.

However, it wasn't the danger in Nigeria that stayed with me the strongest. It was the memories of the people who told me their stories that haunted me. People who hoped I could help them—people I failed by not doing what they thought I could. I remembered all the things I couldn't fit into my reports, or that I let be edited out and didn't fight to keep. It never matters how clearly, and how many times, you explain your role and how limited it is, people believe something more will come from you being there, from you seeing their lives and hearing their stories. They think that somehow telling you their story means you can do something about it. And every time that trust is broken.

Don't get me wrong, the stories of danger were fun for a while, and made exciting conversation at bars back in Australia. But it was cycling home afterwards through the city streets, alcohol buzz wearing off, that the ghosts of those I had betrayed came back to me: Jeffrey, who kept believing the government would one day keep its promises; Kempare, who wanted a job so he could buy his neighbour a bed; and Elekute, the Oporoza leader, who thought speaking to yet another foreigner would somehow, this time, lead to justice for his people.

Darfur, Sudan
Introduction

Darfur is the western region of Sudan, bordering Chad to the west, Libya to the North and the Central African Republic (CAR) to the South. Darfur is made up of three states, North Darfur, South Darfur, and West Darfur.

While there has been conflict in Darfur since the 1980s related to unequal distribution of power and basic service provision, it was around 2001 that a more organised rebellion developed. This rebellion was led, at that time, by the Justice and Equality Movement (JEM) and the Sudan Liberation Army (SLA), comprised mainly of Fur, Zaghawa and Masalit ethnic groups. In 2003, the SLA and JEM joined forces to attack Khartoum, the capital of Sudan. The Sudanese Government responded ruthlessly, recruiting militias and paramilitaries to fight the rebels. 2003 and 2004 were particularly marked by widespread destruction in Darfur with over 200,000 people were killed, and the same number driven into Chad. Another 1.5 million were displaced within Darfur, fleeing to camps for internally displaced persons.[1] The Darfuri rebel groups splintered and multiplied and the conflict continued leading to more deaths and displacement, although not at the same level as in those early years.

This was not the only conflict taking place in Sudan—a war between north and south Sudan had been ongoing for twenty years previous, but came to an end in the early years of the Darfur

---

[1]   Flint, Julie; "Beyond Janjawid: Understanding the Militias of Darfur"; 2009; Small Arms Survey, Switzerland. Available from: http://citeseerx.ist.psu.edu/viewdoc/download?doi=10.1.1.168.4626&rep=rep1&type=pdf.

conflict with the CPA being signed in 2005. This agreement did not mention the conflict in Darfur.

In May 2006, the Darfur Peace Agreement (DPA) was signed with one of the rebel factions—SLA Minni Minnawi but other groups refused to sign. Not only did the conflict not cease, but there was also fighting between the different rebel groups linked to the DPA. The African Union Mission in Sudan (AMIS) came in to monitor the peace agreement and was replaced in early 2008 by the joint United Nations African Union Mission in Darfur—UNAMID.

At this time, the Darfur conflict became the focus of a large advocacy campaign in the West, in the form of the 'Save Darfur' movement, which described the conflict as a genocide. There were strongly held views about the effectiveness of the campaign, which drew enormous media attention and large constituencies of young people in Western countries who advocated for an end to the crisis. However, it was ultimately unable to bring peace, security, or basic services to the people of Darfur.

One outcome of the Save Darfur movement was increased media attention and funding for humanitarian aid. Significant numbers of aid workers went to the three Darfur states to support the IDP camps and endeavour to get assistance to remote communities. These aid workers, often working in camps where security was poor, reported seeing the aftermath of massacres, as well as high number of rapes of women who would have to leave camps to collect firewood. Initially, direct attacks on aid workers were rare, although many NGO vehicles were car-jacked, stolen and turned into 'technicals' (armed vehicles), and satellite phones and other equipment were prized for use by either side in the conflict. The number of attacks directly on aid workers, and UN peacekeepers, increased over time, as did kidnappings. Access to camps for aid workers also became more difficult with access being granted and then revoked. Some staff of aid organisations were imprisoned and some expelled from the country. In 2009, following the indictment of President Omar Bashir by the International Criminal Court, 13 international NGO agencies were expelled from Sudan, and a number of national organisations were shut down. Since this time the number of aid workers and the assistance provided has not returned to pre-2009 levels. Media was also suppressed and today there is limited news of the situation in Darfur.

In 2011 and 2012, the UN reported that roughly 180,000 people had returned home, however in 2013 the UN estimated 300,000 people were displaced within Darfur (twice as many as in 2001 and 2002), including 35,000 crossing into Chad and CAR.[2] There are currently an estimated 1.4 million people living in the main IDP camps in Darfur. Thirteen UN peacekeepers have been killed since October 2012 and many aid agencies have evacuated international staff from Darfur due to the insecurity.[3]

---

2   "Humanitarian progress in Sudan, but significant challenges remain"; 08 August 2012; UN Office for the Coordination of Humanitarian Affairs, New York. Available from: http://reliefweb.int/report/sudan/humanitarian-progress-sudan-significant-challenges-remain-enar.

3   "Irin, Briefing: The humanitarian situation in Darfur"; 15 August 2013; IRIN, Nairobi, Kenya. Available from: http://www.irinnews.org/report/98580/briefing-the-humanitarian-situation-in-darfur.

Grade two girl in Al Salaam IDP camp school. Nyala, South Darfur.
©Jess Shaver

A midwife assessing the river crossing during the rainy season between Tulus and Nyala. ©Carmen Crow Sheehan

The Subtle Thread
Roberta Romano

There's a thread you follow. It goes among
things that change. But it doesn't change.
People wonder about what you are pursuing.
You have to explain about the thread.
But it is hard for others to see.

While you hold it you can't get lost.
Tragedies happen; people get hurt
or die; and you suffer and get old.
Nothing you do can stop time's unfolding.
You don't ever let go of the thread.

from *The Way It Is* – William Stafford

I am reminded in these days that there's a thread.

Brian Draper said, "There are times when all we can do is to follow the thread. Through the dark times as well as the light. The hard times as well as the easy. Uphill as well as down. There is something that has brought us to this place. And that leads us on."

I spend most of my days wondering what that thread is for my life. Trying to be sure that I am holding it tightly, that I am not losing it. Trying to be sure that it is a thread of meaning and that my next move, being either professional or personal, remains faithful to it and that I advance with it.

I lived, for a while, in Darfur, Sudan, in the middle of poverty, war, daily fights, political games, families displaced multiple times, children living under cardboard, women violated on the way home, and air strikes. I exploded into a million questions.

What was the thread for those dark eyes I met during hours of interviews? What was it for the ones I saw arriving to the camp with their very (very) few belongings and very (very) tired faces? What was it for the people whose homes and lands were expropriated? The ones used in the name of a bigger political plan?

Could they hold tight to their thread when there were so few options? No freedom of choice to consider life revisions, no time to plan a change or take strategic decisions. No possibility of considering a Plan B, or feeling in control of the present and the future.

What would Ahmed and Faiza reply? What is the thread for their lives? Their bitten, scarred, violated, stretched, squeezed, and displaced lives?

I stop.
I wonder.
I pray.

Then I glimpse something.

What if the thread is just Life, itself? The first breath in the morning and the last one taken in the evening. The things you do to remain alive and, possibly, safe. The things you do to keep your children alive and, possibly, safe. The deep and almost unconscious desire for a new day.

When I landed in Khartoum on 30 December it was hot and dusty. I was picked up at the airport by the security officer of the organisation I worked for. An Austrian guy with a very strong accent. The type of security guy that wears trousers full of pockets and you are sure he keeps knives and compasses in some of them. With his stories, he immediately gave me the impression that I had landed in another world, where, in the name of something I could not yet grasp, the rules of life and death, and basic respect for human dignity, had been turned and twisted into something else. I spent a few days in his house and I learned to like him. In one of those pockets he carried a significant amount of kindness and humour.

In Khartoum, I spent one of the strangest New Year's Eve's of my life. In the Big House of the organisation's Country Director I found myself among people I didn't know, with experiences I couldn't share, toasting something I could not yet understand.

Welcome to Sudan.

Arriving in South Darfur, a few days later, I had no idea where I was and what I was supposed to do. Of course, before leaving Italy, I had read the most renowned literature on the conflict and I certainly knew where I was standing on a map of the world. But war is not something you can ever be easily familiar with.

Understanding who the victims are, or who the perpetrators are, what are the underlying reasons for taking decisions that lead to death and despair, or how to restore peace and dignity—and quickly—is never easy or immediate. I thought I would come to understand with time, but over time I would discover that the longer you spend in Darfur the less you really know. The more it confuses you, the more you cling to the thread and hope not to lose your way.

I spent two years in Nyala, the capital of the state of South Darfur. While my friends were busy working in camps for internally displaced people delivering food and providing relevant services like water, health care, shelter, or reaching out to displaced communities in more remote and dangerous locations, controlled by rebels at risk of air attacks, I would spend most of my time attempting to find the best ways to prevent and stop human rights violations.

Yes, in the midst of a war perpetrated by the government against minority groups through proxy armies directly attacking civilians, and rebel groups fighting them using the same tactics in return, and in which senior officials would implement their detailed plans for displacement, mass killings and re-shaping of the ethnic distribution of the state, we would spend a significant time sitting and talking to find strategies to prevent or stop human rights violations. Invariably, we were forced to work with the government officials to address the abuses that they themselves were usually perpetrating. It was like knocking at the door of the thief's house, asking permission to enter, identifying the stolen goods and waiting patiently for him to decide whether to give them back to you.

Daily, we would observe the movements of people and groups in order to manage a future return and relocation processes. We asked them, and ourselves, did they decide to move freely? Why did they move? Did they want to go back to where they came from? Would they be able to do it? What happened to their properties and lands when they left? Was this a land grab? By whom? Will they be safe here? Are they even from Darfur?

I came to believe that most movements were triggered as part of a larger and well-defined plan. Entire villages would be displaced by attacks. They would move to a nearby area, and then they were displaced again, and again, and often they would finally reach an IDP camp on the outskirts of a main town. If they were lucky they only ended up losing their properties, houses, and lands. Most, however, would lose family members along the way. While they were gone other people would move in from somewhere else to occupy the 'abandoned' land. Sometimes with both state assistance and support.

Did these people want to be displaced? No. Did they want to abandon their land? No. Did they want to live in four square meters within an IDP camp? No.

I met many of these people personally. I talked to men, women and children (the latter most able to acknowledge and share the truth). I believed that with good and clear evidence we could conduct some effective action to protect them. I thought we could defend these people's rights to move freely and return to their homes. I thought we could repair this situation that had gone so badly wrong. So we carried documents of international relevance: treaties signed by the Government of Sudan, internationally recognised principles. We thought we could just sit on the other side of a government official's desk and convince them to cooperate with us to stop a situation which denied others their basic human rights, freedom, physical security and dignity.

And we believed it was possible; we tried hard. We explored different strategies, new negotiation techniques, different bargaining offers, repeating over and over again the same things. We were threatened both openly and subtly and we consoled ourselves, and justified the value of our work, saying that we were conducting a work of 'protection through presence'. It was our way of saying that without us things would have been worse. Was it true? I still like to believe so.

The second year I was there, when I had grown familiar with the place and stronger in managing my professional objectives, when I could enter the office of a UN agency or a government office and be recognised and listened to, when I had found my place in the midst of the dust and gotten to know everything about the life of our house guard, it was then that I met the man of my life. By that time, I had started wondering seriously and constantly about the sense of what I had seen and known, about the thread I was trying to identify and hold and the one of people I had met on my way, whose rights I was supposed to stand for. I met him in one of those frequent parties aid workers held to keep themselves sane. The ones that began at around 3pm and ended around dark so everyone could get home—into their own walled off compounds —before curfew. We met again at weekly coordination meetings where we used to be briefed on new events and created task forces and working groups to deal with serious issues and to find strength by being together. It was there that we smiled at each other.

After a couple of months, we were sharing the same house, the same sweet dog, the same Friday morning breakfast. Every evening I would go back home to the biggest hug I have ever had from the arms of that generous man, who was brave and resilient enough to become my husband a few years later. In that house, in those days, we mostly talked and talked, and shared the sense of frustration and under-achievement that plagued us all.

It was there that we compared our threads and tied them together and together we grew stronger in a renewed desire to try again the next day, to keep hope for humankind alive even when everything around us tried to extinguish it. We truly believed that despite the dying and the suffering, maybe Life could actually stand a chance of winning in the end.

By the end of my experience in Darfur, I had written hundreds of reports and several policy papers, full of recommendations to be urgently considered by, well, someone. It was not always clear who. I had interviewed thousands of people whose faces were full of dignity, fear, and hope. I had held hundreds of meetings with whoever was available and wanted to coordinate and work with us in pursuit of the difficult, but urgent, mandate of protecting people from forced movements and facilitating their returns home, when possible. I had met with government officials at least once a week, struggling within myself to tell the truth, but in such a way as to avoid expulsion from the country.

Hundreds of thousands of people had died in Darfur and the war continued. It still continues today.

By the time I left, I was not sure that I had made a difference in people's lives—in the lives of Darfuri victims of an unfair and unjust war (is there any just war, after all?). I know I often did my best and sometimes I did not.

There are many things I regret.

I did not speak the truth with the conviction and strength the truth deserves.

I did not work hard enough to find alternative and more creative ways to deal with the situations that were brought to our attention.

I did not feel strongly enough inside me the pain of the victims and their cry for justice, cessation of violence, and restoration of human dignity.

I failed to see, in those I considered the perpetrators, the humanness of their beings, the human identity that goes beyond the acts of violence.

In all my thousands of conversations I never asked Faiza, or Ahmed, what the thread was for them. I was scared to face the answer to that difficult question from someone who had so few options. And so I cannot say with any surety what that thread is for those dark eyes and those tired faces that I met in the midst of the desert. I have not shared their difficult destiny; I have not seen what they have seen and suffered what they have suffered. I have never struggled for survival and never felt that my personal safety and the safety of my loved ones was at risk like theirs. What do I really know about them? About their desire for a new day? About their attempt to hold on to this subtle thread as tight as possible?

In spite of that, I do know that Life was, and is, the only answer to the thousands of questions we asked of ourselves and others. What I know is that I have been confronted, in a very real way, with the fragility of life and the universal value of human dignity. I am probably still the same privileged and idealistic aid worker I was then. Still making my plans and thinking about my next move. However, I see better now and I have learned to recognise the subtle thread—at the heart of all things—that communes us all.

So, what to do now? How to live?

If the thread is Life, and I strongly believe it is, what to do?

Hold it tightly.
Love it.
Respect it.
Stand for it.

Everywhere, every time, with all of yourself.

I Know What Fear Tastes Like
Kelsey Hoppe

I know what fear tastes like. It is small and gritty and metallic—like a rock in your mouth that you cannot spit out and you cannot swallow. It tastes like iron. It tastes like blood.

***

I hadn't meant to run into her. Colleen. I just did. In Nairobi. I was in a shopping centre buying mayonnaise for a friend who still lived in Sudan where mayonnaise was scarce. Colleen was going to the bookshop after work. Both of us had left our jobs in Darfur a year before.

"I spent four months depressed after Darfur," I said in the coffee shop where we had sat down to catch up. "I didn't know how to be depressed. It was new for me."

She held up the number six with her fingers. "Six months. I was depressed for six," she said.

***

I think that I have some sort of selective amnesia. I cannot remember things. I try. At times I practice. I will my mind to remember a face, or a place, or a moment. But it is a fruitless exercise. My mind is already too filled up with more recent people and places and so despite my best efforts I know that—this moment —I will forget.

I will forget Nairobi, and running into Colleen just like I had forgotten her completely the moment I left Darfur. I had forgotten her story until she was in front of me again and my mind had no choice—like a foot-dragging teenager—but to remember. As she walks away my mind turns tail and runs. I look down at the jar of mayonnaise in my hand. I will forget that I was here. Forget what it was like to be me here like I have forgotten what it was like to be me in Darfur. In a few years, someone somewhere at a cocktail party will ask me what Darfur was like and I'll knock at the now-closed door of the sulky teenager. "Dear? Are you in there?" But there will be no answer, just a keep out sign on the door and the music turned up louder. So, I'll shrug, smile benignly and say, "really interesting."

This sort of amnesia is not always bad. It keeps your heart from breaking continually at the enormity and beauty of the world, at the evil you have experienced, and the sheer weight of living. This amnesia folds up the ordinary days into neat bundles, slides them under that door and forgets them so that you can keep living.

***

Colleen had been in Gereida. Everything bad that happened in Darfur was an 'incident'. It was never a murder, an execution, a rape, a hijacking, or a stoning. No. These incidences eventually came to be tagged with monikers: Gereida. Deleige. The WES incident, 19th January.

'Gereida' was significant because of its brutality against NGOs themselves. Unlike in previous incidences, NGOs were not caught in the middle of someone else's fight; a rebel group turned its weapons on the aid workers themselves. In one intense, all night fight that rebel group attacked compounds in which NGO workers lived and worked, stole 13 vehicles, thousands of dollars of communications equipment, attacked Sudanese staff, and staged a mock execution. Some NGOs left after that. Some staff never recovered. Colleen described spending the night laying on the floor of her office while grenades fired from rockets thudded into their compound's concrete walls and the noise of shots and the screams of other colleagues came in over the radios.

Staff of NGOs started talking afterwards about 'acceptable levels of risk' that our NGO would be willing to sustain before we would go as well. However, we'd already had things stolen, colleagues raped, vehicles hijacked, staff killed. If we suddenly said that the risk was unacceptable what did that say about those who'd already been sacrificed? About the risks we'd already accepted and paid for?

We liked to think that our lives, and time in Darfur, were not defined by these incidences but they were. It was by them that we measured time and the length of time that people had been there. "Well, remember Gereida," someone would say. And if you had been there long enough you did. Gereida became the byword for all that could go badly wrong.

***

I smoked a lot in Darfur. To get rid of the taste of the fear. To have something else to do after a security meeting when we stood around useless in the face of what we had just been told. In the face of atrocities we stomached with passive faces, pens at the ready, twice a week:

"22nd, 15.00 hours. North of Cesseban. Several boys who drove donkey carts were approached by a group of unknown armed men. One of the boys escaped and went for help in the local village. When the villagers returned they found that the boys had been chopped into pieces and scattered around."

There was nothing the mind could do with such knowledge. I wrote it down. I reported it. But my mind could not accept it. I simply could not live with it. So I smoked and tried not to taste the fear that was always at the back of my tongue. The taste of helplessness and blood.

***

The psychologist kept asking me the same question after I described each incident. After I put words to Gereida, 19 January, and Deleige. "Yes, but how does that make you *feel?*" The problem was that nothing made me feel anything. It was just a story, a memory that I could so easily forget. I rolled the rock around in my mouth. It felt like nothing. It only tasted.

A taste, however, is not what the psychologist was looking for as she persisted in pushing me to find words to attach to events.

Eventually, I just made one up. It was what, I imagined, everyone did eventually: realised that there must be appropriate words attached to what one had seen or experienced and those words would help someone else understand them. But I didn't have the words so I made them up.

"I felt sad," I said searching her face for some sort of approval. She nodded and scribbled. "And angry," I added.

"Hmmm, good," she said.

"And what was *underneath* that anger?" she continued.

This was never going to end. She could not understand. The entire exercise was a waste of time. There was nothing more.

"More anger?" I guessed and looked out the window at the clear blue London sky.

***

Deleige started simply enough, as all 'incidences' do. A phone call—it was years before I could hear a phone and not expect bad news, not expect to hear someone calmly explain that someone is missing, dead or dying.

Seth called and said that something might have gone wrong in Deleige, a camp in West Darfur where people had fled after their villages were destroyed in the fighting. That's the strange thing about 'incidences'—everyone goes dead calm. Our team had gone into the camp and there was no communication from them. But, there were rumours that had come back that the camp was on fire. He said he couldn't talk longer. I asked if our HQ in the capital had been informed. Yes, he said and hung up.

I sat at my desk and stared out the door into the bright desert heat of an average Darfur afternoon. Everything was still normal in the office. Everything was still normal over that threshold. And it was all about to end. I rolled the rock around in my mouth and told my mind it might want to go to its room for a little while and shut the door. It whined. I told it that it would not like what was about to happen. And I was right. It didn't.

I went to the UN coordination office to ask for a helicopter in case we needed an evacuation and then I went back to the office and I waited. There was no news. No calls. I waited. The security officer of another UN Agency dropped by: "We don't mean to alarm you but we have heard that something might have gone wrong in Deleige camp. We have reports of six people dead." Another UN Agency's security officer came to the office to find out if there was any more information. The representative from the International Red Cross/Red Crescent showed up next as they were doing a food distribution in the same camp and had evacuated. They had no information.

HQ finally called. One driver was dead—Abdul who I had hired just a few weeks ago. Another staff was missing. The vehicles had been torched. The office in the camp: torched.

"Is the death confirmed?" I asked.

"The death is confirmed, the person is not. Do not give out any information on the name until we have gone to the police station and identified the body."

The story emerged slowly. I went to the twice weekly security meeting where it was announced—book-ended by an incident of camel looting and some sort of attack in another camp for displaced people.

"It has been confirmed," the security officer said adding some finality to the sentence that had been left open, "that an NGO has had two vehicles taken and destroyed in Deleige camp. One driver has been killed and several staff are missing." The officer paused and looked at me. It was normal for NGOs involved in security incidences not to be identified in public but given pause at the end of the announcement to add anything they felt relevant. I stared down at my notebook and shook my head. Nothing to add. In truth, we knew far more. Mohammed had been stabbed in the back and head, was beaten and left for dead with Abdul who had been dragged out of the car and executed. Mohammed had been rescued by some local government official and was in and out of a coma and coughing up blood. Musa, who had been with them, had dressed as a woman, as a worker, as anything to escape the mob that chased him from house to house. When some of the sheikhs had tried to protect him the mob had threatened to kill them as well.

It was impossible not to feel guilty. Guilty that I had hired Abdul in the first place. Guilty that he had been executed just for doing the job we had asked him to. Hours later, just after I'd shut up the office and driven home the guard called to me from the gate. Abdul's angry family turned up outside the compound—piling out of pickup trucks—angrily gesticulating and yelling in Arabic. I walked out of the compound gates thinking that they were there to kill me. Perhaps they were. My mind's voice, tiny and weary pounded on the door and told me to go back inside the compound and lock the gate but I could not.

They did not, however, want to stone me. They were angry and they wanted to yell but what they really wanted was to know if their brother, son, and cousin, was dead. And, if he was dead had he been buried in a village nearby the camp, Garsilla, or—contrary to Islamic tradition—would he remain unburied past sundown. He was dead but I couldn't say this. I sent them to find our logistician who could explain everything to them in Arabic and then hurriedly tried to get through to him on the phone that I had just sent an angry mob after him.

It was unclear at that point what should be done and not wanting to sit alone in an empty compound I called a friend who was at the Thursday night party only a few blocks away. She asked if I wanted to come for the few hours between sundown and curfew and I said yes wanting to get out of the way of an angry mob that might be headed back my way.

The party was like most. About a hundred people dancing and drinking themselves into forgetfulness. Someone brought me a glass of Souka, or what we called Janjaweed Juice, a foul smelling, locally brewed date wine that was known to send people straight from sobriety into a three-day hangover.

"I don't drink that stuff," I said.

"I know," she said and handed it to me anyway. "But I think the day you've had might require it." She had a point and so I drank it and the three other glasses that she handed me until I couldn't even remember how I got home.

I did, however, remember puking immediately upon arrival and finding a note by my bed from a colleague who had flown back to the capital that afternoon that read:

"Body will remain buried in Garsilla. Family will be paid. Call Khartoum in the morning. Cheers! Sam"

It is sobering to know that you have sent someone to their death and you have to let your mind out of its room eventually. When you do, you pay for it. I paid for it with insomnia. Lying in bed wrapping and rewrapping a rosary around my hand. Knowing that I was somehow—even inadvertently—responsible for Abdul's death. Knowing that, if we couldn't get a helicopter to fly first thing in the morning that I could be responsible for Mohammed's death as well. A colleague later asked why I was willing to do just about anything for Mohammed—time off, money for his family —anything. I would lie and say it was because I cared but actually, it was because if Mohammed would just simply remain alive it would prove that sometimes, it was enough to save just one. Even if you are the reason they need to be rescued in the first place.

***

In the morning, a helicopter landed, brought in to help us get Mohammed out. I stood there on the tarmac with a UN security officer, shading my eyes from the dust and debris thrown up by the swishing blades.

"You are going to Garsilla?" the pilot asked when the blades finally stopped.

"Well," I said trying to infuse some humour into the situation, "I like to think that 'we're' going to Garsilla."

"Let's go," he said putting his headset back on and handing me one. I shook hands with the German paramedic they'd sent along. He looked about 17 years old.

"Does your mother know you're here?" I asked.

He shrugged and pointed to his head phones to indicate that he couldn't hear a word I was saying. I closed the door as the blades began whipping the ground. Security gave us a thumbs up and headed for their car. I took out a copy of the Guardian that Sam had brought and tried to be nonchalant; tried to pretend that emergency evacuations were just all in a day's work for me. No reason not to keep up with the news. My iPod was plugged in under my helicopter headphones and we flew for an hour over the landscape tinged green by the recent rains.

The German paramedic began gesticulating for me to talk to the pilots through his headset. I put it on. "Where do we land?" the pilot shouted over his shoulder to be heard over the sound of the engines.

"At the World Food Program's airstrip," I yelled back. Could it be that these guys were flying blind? Going somewhere where they had no idea where they were going to land? The helicopter banked hard left and I braced my foot against the first aid box.

"Where is it?" they asked.

"How should I know?" I yelled. "I don't fly here. I'm usually just a passenger. I just know that there's an airstrip. Can't you look for an airstrip?"

"Is that it?" one of the pilots asked pointing down at the WFP food warehouses that had the words WFP painted on the top.

"Ummmm, no," I said. "That's the warehouses…you need to find the airstrip." I tried to keep the rising panic out of my voice. I wasn't even sure that this was Garsilla. If they didn't know where the airstrip was had they checked the coordinates before coming? Wasn't this the age of GPS? This could be Kass or Zalingei. All I knew was that the entire team was waiting for our helicopter in Garsilla with a critically ill man. That Mohammad's life hung in the balance and I, with all the technology in the world and a helicopter, might not be able to get to him.

The pilot spotted a wind sock. I breathed a sigh of relief and we landed.

Seth came over and hugged me ignoring the cultural conventions in Sudan that men and women should not touch in public. We just stood there stupidly hugging on a land strip in the middle of nowhere.

"It's going to be ok, right?" I asked still hugging him and trying not to cry.

"It's going to be ok," he said.

Mohammed looked so small in the stretcher, slight and unconscious. He was loaded in and being attended to by a paramedic. His mother was allowed to come with us and she sat across from me. A poor woman in ragged traditional floral cloth wrapped around her body and over her head. She had probably never ridden in a car much less a helicopter. She gripped her small bag of possessions as if it were life itself. She was blind in one eye and the other cried incessantly. I smiled at her and tried to infuse her with Seth's optimism. It would be ok. I put on her headphones and seatbelt. Her working eye watched me and wept. I turned on my iPod again and listened to Barber's Adagio for Strings over and over and over again as we flew back to Nyala just to hear the violins play a note half way through that sounded so pure and so clear that it, in itself, could keep hope and beauty from disappearing from the world.

***

I looked up from the mayonnaise and around at the busy mall. At Colleen walking away and remembered. Remembered that it would be ok. That sometimes you do save one. Sometimes you swallow that hard pit of fear, that awful truth, and go on. Sometimes you forget your amnesia and you remember. And that is ok too.

No Place
Carmen Sheehan

Darfur is not a place.

Technically, I suppose, it has its own dot on the map. But beyond that, it is not a place. Darfur is a condition. And for those who have come out the other side, it is a marker in time. A coordinate around which their lives are framed.

"Ever since Darfur…"

A sentence with infinite endings.

And mine is this: "Ever since Darfur, I have been haunted by the 'why'."

Why it is acceptable—in anyone's world view—to rape a 10-year-old girl? Why shoot her family in front of her? Why gallop in with AK-47s like the devil on horseback and kill everyone in a village? Or ten villages? Or a hundred? Hell—why commit genocide?

And what makes some people so different from others? How can one man breathe brutality, while the next—of the same religion and tongue—follow to comfort the dying? And what of the survivors? Why him? Why her? Why us?

Ever since Darfur, I have searched for reasons—THE reason. From Laurence Gonzalez to Sun Tzu, and yes, even through JK Rowling's works, I have searched. And like a child with a puzzle that won't quite fit together, I push at the pieces and bend the edges to fit my will. It might be cheating to force together bits that don't fit, but since when did that stop anyone?

*   *   *

This particular day began as they often did for me in Darfur with a text message in the darkness before dawn. Blurry-eyed, I squinted into the blue glow of my Nokia screen. Dr. Hassan—my counterpart—might be late for our staff meeting, he said. Would I mind running it on my own today?

This was unlike him. We always ran these things together; he was the Ernie to my Bert, the Butch Cassidy to my Sundance Kid. More importantly, why couldn't he have waited until dawn to tell me? I groaned, managed to text back a groggy, "OK", and rolled back over under my blanket. The morning had a bite to it.

My Nokia trilled again—a tone that still gives me chills if I hear it on the street today. Another text from Dr. Hassan: "I am in five star hotel of emergency police station," he wrote. "Was picked up round 11pm. Will try to be in the office as soon as I am set free."

Anyone who has spent any sort of quality time in a Sudanese police station would not describe it as a, 'five star hotel'; but here was Dr. Hassan, having himself a good giggle, sending dark humour, at 5:30am, from a crowded concrete cell. He was a rare gem, a genuine Care Bear in the jovial little body of a middle aged Sudanese man. I thought of him there in that awful place, and grasped for the same levity but it eluded me.

* * *

Years later, I found an old copy of *Deep Survival* and at last understood Dr. Hassan's humour. Through harrowing case studies on endurance and death, author Laurence Gonzales recounts the odd tendency of survivors, even in the most horrible situations, to laugh.

> "To deal with reality," he says "you must first recognize it as such, and… play puts a person in touch with his environment, while laughter makes the feeling of being threatened manageable… Because if you let yourself get too serious, you will get too scared, and once that devil is out of the bottle, you're on a runaway horse. Fear is good. Too much fear is not."

I recognise now, what eluded me then, that Dr. Hassan was afraid.

* * *

As soon as I had enough sunlight to safely reach the office, I tracked down our most well-connected staffers: the drivers, of course. They always managed to know things just a heartbeat before the rest of us. It came in pretty damn handy and today was no exception.

The police can arrest anyone they want, the drivers said. And they normally hold them 24 to 48 hours. Last night, the police had launched a wide-scale raid, picking people up 'at random' from the streets. Few things in Darfur, however, were truly random. Dr. Hassan was Zaghawa, one of those ethnic groups long preyed upon by government forces, and was just too tempting a target to pass up.

Was there nothing we could do? I asked.

Nope. Nothing.

So we went about our day. Without Dr. Hassan, I ran the morning staff meeting myself. My voice held steady, even as my heart hammered against my chest. Our meeting closed early as I found it hard to hold my focus between our team travel schedule and Dr. Hassan who had committed the heinous crime—yes, the heinous, heinous crime—of being born to the wrong tribe.

The remainder of the day passed filled with that peculiar blend of bureaucracy and urgency that had come to feel 'normal'. As evening descended, our security officer stopped by with news of a new curfew: 10pm. Also the mobile phone network was down, which couldn't be a good thing. The government cut mobile phone networks when something terrible was about to happen. We were to keep our VHF radio handsets on, he reminded me, and listen for any important updates.

Normally, my house mate Susan and I straggled out of the office at different hours but this evening we clung together—a feeble sense of safety in numbers. We were issued vehicle number seven, a weathered, white Land Cruiser, threw our laptops in the back, climbed side-by-side into the front seat, and drove together to the grey cement compound we called home. Dusk was falling, and the call to prayer echoed from loudspeakers across town. It was both beautiful and lonely, and resonated with the crippled shards of hope still clinging to my core.

Susan disappeared into the seclusion of her room. We had yet to receive news from Dr. Hassan, and the mounting anxiety ran like poison in my blood. I needed to get out, do something, do anything....

We had a couple of hours before curfew and I heard over the radio handset that the head of our logistics department had arrived from Khartoum. He was a nice old fellow, a seasoned aid work veteran, with a mellow presence. Just the sort of company I could use just then. He probably had not been offered any dinner as he was staying at the third of our four guest house compounds. While the usual suspects who lived there were known for many things, hospitality was not one of them.

Jamming the radio handset into the waistband of my jeans, I rummaged around the kitchen looking for something quick and palatable. Onions. Dried lentils. A big plastic jug of cooking oil. Nope, nope, and nope. Finally, I just grabbed a bottle of mango juice and a sleeve of digestive biscuits, and headed out. It wasn't much in the way of food, but it was more than he would be getting from his hosts in Guest House Three. The key was where we normally left it, in the driver's side door—perfect for quick access in case anyone might need to leave in a hurry. Like, the do-or-die sort of hurry, which was known to happen in places like this.

John was in the courtyard of Guest House Three already entertaining our transportation manager at a metal table in the middle of their otherwise concrete world. They pulled up an extra chair and I produced my offering; John rejoiced in the juice and biscuits as if it were Christmas ten times over.

"Sorry," I said, although his smile was radiant, "I didn't have much sitting around."

The wrinkles around his eyes deepened. "Truly. This is perfect." And I think he really meant it.

He and Mustafa were talking shop but I desperately wanted to hear something human. "Tell me about your daughters, John." I wanted to know about his girls, his family, his life back home, far from here. I liked watching how he lit up when he spoke of them. I liked how it made me feel normal, even for just a short while, in a world that was anything but.

John obliged me for a little while with stories from his other life, worlds away from police raids and government curfews, and my worry for Dr. Hassan faded just enough to be almost bearable.

And then we were looking at our watches. 9.30!

Mustafa and John stood with me. We walked to the gate, and the guards flipped on the outside lights as I fumbled for the key. I fired up the engine. Except… it didn't start. A brief mechanical cough, and then silence.

The stillness sent prickles along my skin. Of all the possible times for a vehicle to malfunction, a curfew night was not optimal. I tried again. Still nothing.

Damn.

I climbed back out.

We popped the hood and huddled around the engine. I was a health person. This labyrinth of metal meant nothing to me. But clearly, it spoke to Mustafa and John. They were already tinkering, mumbling back to forth, prodding and poking and shifting things about.

9:34.

One by one, the guards joined in. They whispered suggestions in Arabic; Mustafa nodded and grumbled in turn.

Nervously, I monitored my watch as curfew closed in.

9:38. John glanced up from the engine. "You are welcome to stay here tonight if you need to."

It was nice of him, but I couldn't leave Susan alone without a vehicle. If something happened during the night, she would be trapped. One way or another, I needed to get home… and I had 22 minutes to do it.

9:41.

The Land Cruiser let loose a glorious belch. It didn't sound pretty, but it was alive and that was all I needed. My house was not far. I could make it in five minutes—cutting it close, but it would still be before curfew.

Pouring thanks over the pit crew, I clambered back in behind the wheel.

"I should ride with you past the first checkpoint." Mustafa was already climbing in to the passenger seat. "In case they set up early. I can speak to them in Arabic, and talk you through safely."

"Are you sure?" I glanced at the clock face on the dashboard. "Will you still get home on time?"

"I do not live far. You can let me off after the checkpoint, and I will walk." He fastened his seatbelt. "Come, we should hurry."

John nodded to me from the passenger window. And so I switched on the headlights, shifted into first, and waved over my shoulder as we pulled out.

Typically, there was one checkpoint between Guest House Three and Guest House One, at the bend in the road by the tea shop; I slowed as we approached. But there was no sign of activity. In fact, there was no sign of anything—not a pedestrian, not a vehicle, not so much as a stray donkey.

I slowed to a stop. "No checkpoint," I breathed, trying to ignore the sudden, creepy aura of desolation. "Shall I let you out here?"

"I can ride all the way if you like," offered Mustafa. "I do not live far."

But I knew that was a stretch. He didn't live nearby and the closer we got to my home, the farther we got from his.

"That is very kind of you, Mustafa, but I think it is safe now. I can make it OK from here. Please, go so you can make it home too."

"You're sure?"

"Yes." I dug out a little local lingo. "*Shoukran.*" Thanks.

Mustafa grinned at my fledgling Arabic. "You are welcome. Be safe."

And with that, he hopped out of the car and was gone.

I put my foot back on the gas, and headed for the roundabout.

And straight into the barrels of six AK-47s.

I blinked. And they were still there. Six little demons—high school age at best—braced shoulder to shoulder in the street, training their AK-47s on my windshield.

I must have braked because I was at a full stop, staring into the firing squad. The boys looked edgy. Aggressive.

"Protocol, protocol!" The little security voice in my head spoke evenly. "Turn off your headlights. You're blinding them."

* * *

Laurence Gonzalez also wrote, "Nearly all survivors report hearing what they call 'the voice'. It tells them what to do. It is the speaking, rational side of the brain, the one that processes language, the wellspring of reason."

So, that voice in my head? The voice I wondered about all these years? Apparently, it was perfectly rational. Schizophrenia be damned!

* * *

I turned off my headlights.

"Now turn on the inside cabin light. They're nervous when they can't see you."

I switched on the inside cabin light.

"And remember: It's harder to shoot someone in the face if they're smiling." Thanks for that.

I rolled down the window, leaned out, feigned a smile, and waved. "*Alsalam alaykum!*" Hello!

The streetlights were just strong enough to catch the confusion registered on their faces. Friendly gusto of foreigners speaking Arabic clearly fell outside their standard programme. The boys lowered their weapons. Someone waved for me to pull over.

"Go slowly, now."

I pulled into the spot they indicated, between a taxi and a small car. Apparently I wasn't the only one caught by surprise before 10pm.

I waited for whatever was next, but nothing happened. They left me alone. I glanced at the clock face on the dashboard. 9:48. I should be home by now. Nobody would suspect that I'd been snagged—unless Susan was still awake and noticed I hadn't made it back—and even then, what could she do?

Perhaps the network was back up? Maybe I could send a discreet text? I fumbled for my Nokia phone. The blue glow showed no network and my heart sank.

"Keep your hands visible."

Right! Awkwardly, I draped both hands over the steering wheel. No, that wouldn't work. My hands were trembling too badly. I shifted my arms again; if I braced one along the windowsill and pressed the other against the wheel, my shaking was less obvious. This was better. It would have to do. Someone was coming.

"Don't let them see that you are afraid."

Boots crunched on the gravel.

Just last week, our security briefing had included a sentence on precisely this sort of thing. A woman, caught in a checkpoint after dark. The police had been drunk and assaulted her—attempted rape.

"Keep it together! Focus! Don't let them see your fear."

I watched the man approach. He was older, and in uniform; police or military, I couldn't tell. Did it even matter? I smiled. "*Alsalam alaykum!*" Hello! Surely, he would have to be impressed by my Arabic. I focused on the muscles in my face; relaxed my forehead; stamped back the terror from my eyes. "*Keef halak?*" How are you?

"*Kowais*," he responded. "*El hamdolelaah.*" Good, thanks be to God.

I could see his face now as he drew even with my window, seemingly puzzled by his own auto-pilot response to my pleasantries.

"Keep your seatbelt fastened. It will buy you some time if he tries to drag you out."

He made no move; he just stared, perhaps rightfully so, wondering why this very white khawaja woman was manically smiling at him.

Deeming me no immediate threat—perhaps just a bit loopy— he continued along his way, surveying the other vehicles before coming to rest against the hood of the taxi beside me.

9:59

10:02

The minutes crept by slowly. There we sat. The taxi, the small car, and me. I began to wonder if maybe this random detention that Dr. Hassan and I each faced was simply a power trip—we rule and therefore you wait.

Perhaps some chit-chat would make it easier for them to let me go. Granted, with my limited Arabic, the intellectual range of our conversation would be small but it was worth a shot.

* * *

"If you need something from somebody, always give that person a way to hand it to you," wrote Sue Monk Kidd, in *The Secret Life of Bees*. So with my limited Arabic I took my best shot.

* * *

I leaned out the window, tried to look casual and said to the man leaning on the taxi, "It is cool tonight."

The man looked up. "Eh?"

Once more. In Arabic. "It is cool tonight."

Confusion and curiosity met at the crease in the middle of his brow. "It is."

And we were off.

Never have I been so fluent as I was in that moment. The adrenaline inspired words I never knew I knew. Ten minutes later, we were still going strong. We continued agreeing that the evening was cool, that the days had been hot. His uniform was green. We counted to ten. I asked what time it was. We synchronised our watches.

"Well," I said, shimmying into my grand finale, "I am sleepy."

He looked confused again.

"My home is not far." I pointed. "I would like to go to the home."

Slowly, with a small shrug, he stepped into the road to wave me out. Really? Just like that? Hardly believing my fortune, I released the parking brake and threw the Land Cruiser into reverse.

"Slow and steady, now."

Willing the motor not to die, I backed gently out into the road and glanced in the rear view mirror. If the firing squad in the road kept it together I would be free. So, just to ensure we were all on the same page, I leaned out the window, waved, and wished them all a very splendid evening.

The whole crew—my talkative friend, the boys with the guns, every last one of them—waved back.

And I went home.

* * *

Sun Tzu suggests in *The Art of War,* that, "to overcome others' armies without fighting is the best of skills." While not a military strategist myself, all I could think was, "Amen, brother Tzu. My point exactly."

* * *

The next morning I awoke to the sound of donkey carts rattling past my window, off for their pre-dawn water deliveries. Ah yes. Good morning, Darfur.

Half an hour later, I was dressed and ready. Cloaked in the gentle morning rain along the road to the office, the roundabout had shed any hint of foreboding. Traffic puttered past. Women wandered by with bags for the market. The light of day lent a warm hue to the pavement. It was as if yesterday had never happened.

Except for two things. The network was still down. And there was still no word from Dr. Hassan.

Sometimes, though, the world offers a little gift—the occasional sheepish apology for its cruelty, for what it's put you through. Mine walked in still dressed in a wrinkled, un-tucked dress shirt from two days ago while I was gathering my notes for the morning meeting. Dr. Hassan stood in the doorway. Disheveled, weary, and radiating joy.

"Am I in time for staff meeting?"

Caught somewhere between a laugh and a sob, I managed to smile and nod. Of all the things to say when just out of prison. Yes, Dr. Hassan. You are a day late, but yes.

"Are you okay?"

"I am. *El hamdolelaah.*"

I surveyed for damage but detected only delight. "Can I ask what happened?"

"Oh, the police, you know, they threatened to beat me, they threatened to kill me." He shrugged. "But I told them I'm a doctor and I see death every day. So if they were going to kill me they should just do it and stop wasting my time."

I raised my eyebrows. "And they let you go?"

He held out his arms, as if proof in himself. Which, in fact, he was. "They did."

* * *

It has been years now since I last set foot in the sands of Darfur, but the condition remains with me still. In books, in friends, in the far corners of life, I have continued my search for the 'why'. And I have yet to find it.

The condition is hard to shake. Surely, there must be some explanation. So I continue to go around and around in the maddening cycle of my humanitarian hamster wheel of questioning, and of all the countless sources out there, there is one quote that I keep going back to.

It's by JK Rowling in the last chapter of *Harry Potter and the Goblet of Fire*, where Hagrid sits down with Harry for tea and cookies.

The tragedies of the Triwizard Tournament are still fresh; Harry wonders what more he could have done; the future is grim.

> "You all righ'?" [Hagrid] said gruffly.
> "Yeah," said Harry.
> "No, yeh're not," said Hagrid. "'Course yeh're not. But yeh will be."

I love this scene. Certainly not for the grammar or the spelling, but probably because I want—very much—to believe Hagrid is right.

For Harry.

For me.

For us.

For Darfur.

For the possibility that someday it may shed its darkness, that the condition will have a cure, that I will understand the why, and Darfur will at last become just one more place on a map.

"There Is No Rape In Darfur"
Kirsten Hagon

We bumped along the track in our dusty white Land Rover through farming land, past small round mud brick houses and camels off in the distance, slowing as we neared a herd of goats. The checkpoint was a square thatched building with a dirt porch; a man with an AK-47 in a shabby army uniform ambled out to check our papers. The United Nations flag flapping from the radio antennae was faded to light blue and somewhat tattered. This checkpoint, and more importantly the camp and its inhabitants beyond it, would later become very familiar to me, but at that time it was all so new. The official waved us through and we continued, the Land Rover's wheels deep in the ruts carved into the road by previous aid agency vehicles. The vehicle leaned precariously to one side, continuing in a direction parallel to the train tracks, until we reached the edge of Kalma camp.

It was 2006 and this was the largest camp in Darfur for persons displaced by the conflict, described as internally displaced persons. This title indicated that they were Sudanese displaced within Sudan as opposed to refugees who had come from another country. If they had been refugees they would have (in theory) had more rights, but as IDPs, the government was both their persecutor and their supposed protector.

Kalma was no standard IDP camp. This was a city. A city of 90,000 people. This camp was one of the largest refugee or IDP camps in the world.[1] It was an emergency home to people of many different

---

1   The camp has since been split into smaller camps.

ethnicities, from multiple locations. Families were squashed into one-room tents or mud brick shelters with ripped plastic or fabric sheet doorways flapping in the wind. The more rudimentary of these tents were squat-domed structures of woven branches piecing together the pink and yellow sacks that once carried grain. Barely a meter in diameter, they were impossible to stand up in. Other shelters were larger, with mud-brick walls and white UN-logoed plastic sheets over the roof to keep out the rain. There were also market stalls made of low, mud-brick or bundled-stick walls with woven grass and twig roofs, called racubas.

I hadn't really known what to expect; I didn't see the conditions as particularly bad or good as I had nothing to compare them to. I felt merely the excitement of being somewhere new, of finally doing the work I had wanted to do for so many years. Accompanying the excitement was the nervousness that my previous experience was somewhat meaningless here, in the context of ongoing conflict. How relevant would my years of legal training be amidst all this impunity and war, where civilians are the pawns abused in struggles over land and resources?

Once we drove past the first NGO run medical clinic and into the camp the scene changed. We saw men with bright smiles in long white *jallabeyas*[2] and white turbans. Some were riding or wheeling bicycles in the sand, some walking in flip-flops or hyena-patterned slippers. We saw women wrapped in brightly coloured pieces of fabric known as taubs, which began at their waists, forming a skirt and then wrapped sari style around their upper bodies with the end

---

2   Loose long white robes worn by Darfuri men.

draped loosely over their heads. We passed these women standing in line to fill yellow, plastic jerry cans with water or walking carrying large bundles of sticks for firewood on their heads. Children with bare feet and large grins were running after us, waving and calling out '*khawaja, khawaja*'—foreigner, foreigner. A donkey drawn cart plowed slowly beside us, filled with more brightly dressed women from the camp.

All these were sights that would soon become familiar to me, as I visited the camp and our projects there each week, sometimes two or three times. I got to know well the small, open-air market with the larger squarer buildings where men were working busily on sewing machines under the shade of grass mat roofs. Nearby women sold firewood in piles on the sand, while others had small stalls selling neat pyramids of tomatoes, furry cucumbers by the piece, small withered onions and sand-covered bunches of leafy greens.

There were NGO health clinics, women's centres, and youth centres surrounded by grass fences or a low, mud-brick wall. There was a larger compound with an iron sheet fence and a large shady open roofed structure under which the community leaders— Sheikhs or Omdas, and the women Sheikhas—would meet and debate for hours issues of camp management, security and so on. A huge UN World Food Program warehouse sat at the edge of the camp piled high with sacks of millet that made up the regular food distributions. Nearby there was a post manned by African Union peacekeepers.

The inhabitants of Kalma were from all over the state of south Darfur and sometimes beyond. They were mainly people that the government-allied militias had violently forced from their lands. They had walked for days or weeks to reach Kalma, just outside the capital city of South Darfur—Nyala. There were four main ethnic groups and many more groups of smaller numbers, including the occasional southern Sudanese. They spoke multiple and differing languages, and many were from isolated rural communities with little education. My patchy Arabic was of minimal use, in particular with the women, whose lack of formal education meant that few of them spoke any Arabic, but instead spoke Fur, Zhaghawa, Massalit, or other local languages.

Kalma was not only the largest IDP camp in Darfur but also the most controversial. The majority of Kalma residents were from tribes that opposed, or were at least perceived to oppose, the government. The Sheikhs that had been displaced to Kalma were some of the most well known and influential in Darfur. It was Kalma that was also most often in the Western media. It was Kalma that the then-UN Emergency Relief Coordinator and Undersecretary General for Humanitarian Affairs, Jan Egeland, visited in 2005 and 2006, angering the government when he demanded that the government officials stay outside while he met the Sheiks. It was here, in May 2006, that an interpreter working for the African Union Peacekeeping Mission was killed and a number of peacekeeping personnel injured when camp residents protested against the Darfur Peace Agreement, which they viewed as illegitimate because only one faction of those who opposed the government had signed the Agreement.

Against this fraught backdrop, the government viewed Kalma as a threat. There were many altercations between government police and Kalma residents. Kalma residents complained about police abuses until, in 2006, they effectively threw the police out of the camp. Jokingly, Kalma was from this point onwards often referred to by the aid workers as, 'the independent republic of Kalma'.

I understood little of these politics when I arrived. This was my first 'field' assignment so my first role was to listen, learn, and work out what I was meant to do in this new and alien place. I was here to work on a rule of law programme—a title which made some people snigger given the context. My particular focus was on women victims of crimes under Sudanese law (based on an interpretation of Islamic Sharia Law), in particular rape, and those accused of adultery. Adultery is considered a crime under Sudanese criminal law, and an unmarried woman who becomes pregnant is often presumed guilty of adultery and can be punished by lashing. For a married woman, the punishment is death by stoning.

My first discussions with Kalma residents were about their issues of immediate concern: Violence in and around the camp, problems with the food, the lack of soap, the need for more plastic sheeting, the fear of the oncoming rainy season, which would turn the roads to rivers of mud. Food rations in Kalma, camp residents informed me, were far from ideal. They were not culturally appropriate, they did not include meat, or other items that people wanted and needed. The grain provided had to be milled before it could be used in cooking. A significant percentage was sold or traded for other things people needed, or simply to raise the money to mill their remaining grain. There were also families that said they had been in the camp for months but without any rations because they had been unable to register their presence with the relevant agencies.

There was limited work available, and finding sources of income to pay for additional items like meat, soap, and fuel for cooking stoves was a challenge. Women complained that the men in their families couldn't find work and so they had to look for income. This reversal of gender roles brought with it various challenges—in terms of impact on the men's self esteem, excessive time they had difficulty filling (which some would deal with by drinking locally brewed alcohol), and high rates of domestic violence in the camp.

Women could earn the much-needed income by selling firewood. The women of Kalma would venture out into the desert landscape around the camp to cut small trees and brush to use and sell. As the area became more deforested the women would venture further into increasingly dangerous territory. They told me of the sexual assaults they had survived. Mothers, pregnant women, grandmothers, children—no one was safe when they went out to collect firewood.

Their stories painted a horrific picture, but one that should not have surprised me. As a refugee lawyer in Egypt, I had listened to the experiences of numerous women and child refugees—experiences involving rape in war and torture—but these were told after the fact, when they were generally 'safe' and it was unlikely to happen again. But here, the women lived with the knowledge that this could likely happen again. When I asked the women why they were collecting firewood and not their husbands, the response was that the women would 'only' be raped, whereas their husbands would be killed.

According to the women the perpetrators were *Janjaweed* grazing their cattle.[3] They were armed, and some of them were wearing military uniforms. The rapes were to humiliate and the perpetrators spoke about the ethnicity of the victims, calling them 'slaves'. Few of the women wanted to report to the police. Indeed, the police had in the past laughed at women who reported rapes or arrested them for adultery.

We called these incidents, euphemistically, 'protection threats'. I began to understand what people meant when they talked about a 'protection gap', although it might have been better described as a complete absence of any protection for these women from the threats they faced.

The week I arrived, a meeting was held with a large group of Kalma women and some of the international aid agencies. Despite the cultural shame linked to rape (not to mention legal implications as women could be accused of adultery or forced to marry the perpetrator to avoid family shame), the women were vocal about what was happening to them. They reported that over a period of ten days some 100 women were raped collecting firewood outside Kalma camp. An NGO press release at the time reported that 200 women from Kalma had been raped in a five-week period.[4]

---

3   Literal translation: 'devils on horseback', the term used to describe the government-allied militias who often attacked villages.
4   "Aid agency warns on Darfur rapes"; 24 August 2006; BBC News. Available from: http://news.bbc.co.uk/2/hi/africa/5280286.stm.

The UN later described this as a 'massive upsurge of rape' around Kalma camp.[5] With numbers so staggering, it appeared to me that there was nothing random to this violence.

There had been various initiatives in the past to increase the security of these women. The introduction of cooking stoves that slowed firewood consumption was lauded in front of the Western government donors as the answer to the prayers of these women. If their fuel lasted longer then this would, in theory, reduce the need to venture out of the camp for firewood. However, this did nothing to prevent attacks when women still had to go, and completely ignored the fact that the reason women left the camp was more because of their need for some sort of income than it was for firewood as fuel for personal use.

The African Mission in Sudan (AMIS) peacekeepers started to undertake firewood patrols where the AMIS civilian police would go out with the women to provide some level of protection from the threat of attack. However, this was less than perfect; the women told me that, at times, the soldiers didn't turn up due to insecurity, or impassable muddy roads, or that they accompanied the women to the site and then left before the women had returned. Having no interpreters the peacekeepers were unable to communicate with the women to address these challenges. Some initiatives were undertaken to identify interpreters and to establish standard procedures, but invariably peacekeeping personnel would rotate out and the women would be back to square one with the incoming personnel.

---

5   Joint UN Media release, 9 October 2006

So the prevention of these incidents was far from ideal, but then neither was the response after the fact. Rape survivors need to get medical assistance immediately in order to deal with life threatening injuries and to take medication to prevent pregnancy and HIV/ AIDS. In Kalma, these medical clinics existed; however, women were often too scared to visit them. I later learned that the medical personnel in some of the clinics, in particular government clinics, were also too scared to treat rape victims, or if they did would do so secretly and not fill out the required paperwork that might support a legal case. Women were not always treated well at medical clinics, and at times reported that doctors had accused them of fabricating their stories to cover adultery.

Legal processes were an enormous challenge, and often attempting to engage in these could cause more harm than good. Women who reported rape were often ostracised by their families and communities. And, they had to contend with a legal system that generally viewed them, rather than the perpetrators, as having broken the law.

Getting the right documentation was the first hurdle of any legal process. In court, a document known as 'Form 8' was required as evidence of rape. Headed, "Form to accompany the person, or the body, for medical examination", both a police officer and a doctor were supposed to fill it out for anyone who had been physically or sexually assaulted, or killed. Form 8 however, was rarely present in either police stations or medical clinics. Women reported to their lawyers being required to pay to have the form filled out or the police would later claim the form hadn't been completed.

In the end, the situation was one of overwhelming impunity. A UN press release in October 2006 said, "The rising rate of violence against women and children is increased by the participation of many different groups in these crimes… there is scant evidence that culprits are being actively sought, let alone punished, for their crimes."[6] More women might have faced the daunting task of pressing charges had there been any prospect of success or belief that the perpetrators would be brought to justice. Some women were courageous and did take this step. During my time in Darfur there were less than a handful of successful prosecutions for rape, but each one was considered a victory.

The major barrier to preventing and responding to the rapes was politics: politics being played out over women's bodies. In Darfur, to say a woman was raped was somehow a political act. The Sudanese government consistently denied incidents and refuted statements made by the UN, or NGOs, and reported in international media. They argued that any reports of rape were untrue unless they had been proved in court, but then they made it nearly impossible to get a case to court. At a memorable speech on International Women's Day in late 2006, the Minister for Women's Affairs in South Darfur said that rape had never existed in Darfur before the international humanitarian community came, and that it was them that brought rape to Darfur.[7]

In this context we would often debate our role as humanitarians. Was our role simply to provide services to those who survived

6   "UN Condemns Massive Upsurge in Rapes in Darfur"; 9 October 2006. UNICEF, New York. Available from: http://www.unicef.org/media/media_36107.html.

7   Based on translation of the speech (not publicly available)

(medical, legal, counselling, to reduce exposure to risk through alternative income sources), and through quiet means to do all we could to prevent similar attacks from occurring again? Or was our role to bear witness, to tell the world what was going on, again with the hope this could prevent future violations? This latter approach was controversial and risky for the organisations and individuals involved. Staff in Sudanese NGOs risked arrest and indeed were often detained. Staff at international organisations had to grapple with the consequences of being kicked out of the country. If we weren't there, who would provide basic services to the people who needed them? But if we didn't speak out, were we somehow complicit?

Following the numerous attacks in mid-2006, the UN approached the Deputy Governor of South Darfur to bring his attention to the increasing insecurity around Kalma camp, especially for women. Rather than responding to the concerns raised, the Deputy Governor denied the reports and used the moment to undertake an 'investigation' of the NGO responsible for camp management. Within two months the organisation was expelled from Darfur. The Deputy Governor later gave a speech to the Human Rights Council in Geneva where he stated: "There are continued attempts to spread fabricated information about cases of rape in Darfur and about the scale of this phenomenon. Inquiries led by the UN, AU and GOS have proven that the exaggerated claims of a European NGO, which has been expelled from Sudan, were absolutely incorrect. The Government has adopted a robust plan to eradicate violence against women that will be implemented with all required attention." This NGO had never actually put out any media reports on the issue. What was happening to the women of Kalma was the real issue, this was pure distraction.

This wasn't the first or the last time this had happened. In 2005, two employees from another NGO, *Medecins Sans Frontieres,* were arrested and charged with espionage and publishing false information. Their arrest occurred after they had issued a report detailing the rapes of hundreds of victims they had treated in Darfur hospitals.[8] More recently, in 2009, 13 aid organisations were expelled from Darfur. This happened immediately after the International Criminal Court indicted the Sudanese president for war crimes. The Sudanese government claimed these organisations had been, "giving information to the ICC," which all of the organisations denied.

We as the humanitarian community were able to provide medical assistance, legal aid and other forms of care to some of these women. But now, some six years later, I wonder if any of the structures built, or systems developed, have had any sustained impact. It has been a long time since I last visited the camp, passed the checkpoint or the NGO centres, or talked to the women in the heat and dust under the shade of a racuba. I wonder if the women of Kalma are in any way safer now than they were when I left Darfur in 2007. How far afield do they now venture to collect firewood to sell?

As noted in 2009 in a news article referring to the expulsion of the aid agencies:

---

8   Médecins Sans Frontières, "The Crushing Burden of Rape - Sexual Violence in Darfur"; 8 March 2005; MSF Briefing Paper, Amsterdam. Available from: http://www.doctorswithoutborders.org/publications/reports/2005/sudan03.pdf

With the void left by the ousted organizations, the
United Nations has instituted emergency measures to
help provide food, water, and other vital aid. But one
service remains virtually decimated: support for rape
survivors.[9]

I notice these days there is almost nothing in the news about
Darfur; nothing in the news about the women of Kalma; nothing
in the news about rape in Darfur. I wish I believed it was because
the women of Kalma are safe. But in this case I do not think that
no news is good news. It is simply a sign that we are absent, and
that the few humanitarians who do remain, the local civil society
organisations, and the women themselves, remain too scared to
speak out.

---

9   Hamilton, Rebecca; "Why aid for Darfur's rape survivors has all but disappeared", 14 October
2009, The New Republic. Available from: http://www.newrepublic.com/article/world/left-behind.

Malawi, nestled in a narrow band of land between Mozambique, Tanzania, and Zambia, is a culturally conservative, landlocked, densely-populated country. Formerly a British colony, Malawi gained independence in 1964 and enjoyed relative stability and solid relations with both its African neighbors and the West over the next 40 years, first under single-party rule and then under a multi-party democracy instituted in 1994.[1] Attractions such as its 500km-long, freshwater lake, the elephant and hippo populations of Liwonde National Park, and its reputation as the 'Warm Heart of Africa' provides a boon to the local economy through tourism.

Malawi is among the poorest countries in the world with more than 50% of the population living below the poverty line and a ranking of 170 out of 187 countries on the United Nations' Human Development index—a broad measure of a country's health, education and income.[2] Of Malawi's approximately 15 million people, 45 percent are under the age of 14 years and 74 percent live in rural areas.[3]

Social and health indicators in Malawi are poor. Although more than 76 percent of children attend primary school, only approximately 20 percent attend secondary school.[4] In 2011, there

1   Republic of Malawi (Constitution) Act, 1994
2   World Bank. 2010. Available from: http://data.worldbank.org/country/malawi.; UNDP Malawi Country Profile: Human Development Indicators. 2012. Available from: http://hdrstats.undp.org/en/countries/profiles/MWI.html.
3   UNdata Country Profile: Malawi. 2012. Available from: http://data.un.org/CountryProfile.aspx?crName=MALAWI.
4   UNICEF: Country Profile: Malawi. 2011. Available from: http://www.unicef.org/infobycountry/malawi_statistics.html.

were only approximately 3,800 nursing and midwifery personnel and 257 physicians serving the entire country.[5] An average woman in Malawi will give birth six times, which contributes to both high maternal and infant mortality.[6] Life expectancy in Malawi is 54 years.[7]

Not all is bleak in Malawi. Although approximately 12 serving the entire country of the population is infected with HIV, over the last five years Malawi successfully expanded HIV/AIDS prevention, treatment and care programmes throughout the country.[8] By 2013, more than 420,000 patients were managed on life-saving antiretroviral medications for HIV-infection in almost 700 clinics, a tremendous achievement in large part supported through the United States' Presidents Emergency Plan for AIDS Relief (PEPFAR).[9]

Recent political turmoil in Malawi threatened critical donor investment. In 2010, relations between Malawi and several of its Western donors began to deteriorate over financial and human rights concerns under second-term President Bingu Wa Mutharika. Things worsened significantly in July 2011 when both the UK and U.S. suspended aid over growing concerns about government intimidation of civic demonstrators, restrictions on press freedom, and increasing police violence.[10] Upon the sudden

5   World Health Organization. 2011. "World Health Statistics." Available from: http://www.who. int/whosis/whostat/2011/en/index.html.
6   UNICEF: Country Profile: Malawi. 2011, op.cit.
7   Ibid.
8   National Statistical Office Malawi. 2011. Malawi Demographic and Health Survey 2010. Calverton, MD, NSO and ORC Macro.
9   Government of Malawi, Ministry of Health. 2013. Integrated HIV Program Report: January – March 2013. Lilongwe, Malawi.
10   Dugger, Celia. "U.S. Freezes Grant to Malawi Over Handling of Protests. " New York Times, July 26, 2011. Available from: http://www.nytimes.com/2011/07/27/world/africa/27malawi. html?_r=0.

death of President Mutharika in April 2012, then-Vice President Joyce Banda, took over as Africa's second, and Malawi's first, female President. Restoring civic freedoms, replacing officials blamed for the shortages and violence, and gaining back the trust of the foreign donors who fund much of Malawi's national budget have been priorities.[11] As of 2013, Malawi appears back on track for political, social, and financial improvements.

---

11   Tenthani, Rafael. 2012. "Joyce Banda: Malawi's first female president." BBC News Africa, April 10, 2012. Available from: http://www.bbc.co.uk/news/world-africa-17662916. [Accessed September 15, 2013].

Carrying bundles of long-lasting insecticide treated (LLIN) mosquito nets during a distribution campaign in partnership with PSI in Western Bahr el Ghazal, South Sudan. ©Jenn Warren

Women with long-lasting insecticide treated (LLIN) mosquito nets during a distribution campaign in partnership with PSI in Western Bahr el Ghazal, South Sudan. ©Jenn Warren

Inside the crowded hangars at Songore Transit Camp. Built to host 70 people, the hangars at Songore hold 150 or more Rwandans each. Many families are building private straw huts, and others must sleep outside because of lack of constructed hangars. ©Jenn Warren

Home Is Where The Hard Is
Caryl Feldacker

From 8,000 miles away, on his fourth multi-week home leave of the year, my fiancé, Andy, unceremoniously dumped me over a crackly Skype connection. He had been gone several weeks with little contact, attending two weddings, hanging out with his best friends, enjoying the feasts and freedom of the U.S.

I, on the other hand, was at our home in Malawi. Alone, again, and anxious about staying by myself with continued civil unrest. The increasingly frequent power cuts meant an even more sporadic internet connection, limiting my contact with the outside world. Fuel pumps everywhere were dry, prohibiting any non-work related travel. I was frazzled. Over the previous month, I had sent him several lengthy emails and received pithy replies signed off with, gotta run! I asked him to find time to Skype-chat, but Andy kept noting how hard it was to find a computer when not traveling with one. I had asked him to purchase a phone card so he could call me on his cell, but he said they were expensive. Finally, three days before he was supposed to return, we finally connected over Skype. Through muffled words, several power cuts, long delays, and an echo louder than the initial words, I heard this, twice: "our relationship is unsalvageable."

Unsalvageable: a gut-wrenching, four-word verdict declaring that everything between us was worthless beyond repair. My immediate thought? Not, "I'll miss him;" not "I love him;" not "What will I do without him?" Rather, "Crap! Now we'll have to Photoshop him out of my nephew's Bar Mitzvah photos!"

Obviously, this abrupt end was not a complete surprise. I had been trying to hold everything together—my job, my relationship with this man, living in this country—for the remaining six months of my contract. I was sure that once we returned to the U.S., everything would return to normal. But, Andy bailed first; he was saving himself. At the time, I viewed it as him giving up. I, on the other hand, was not a quitter: I worked in international health. I dug in and moved things forward no matter how hopeless the situation was. If life, or the market, handed me moldy lemons, I would force them into a lemon tart with lemon zest. I looked on the bright side. Ultimately, this break up was the bright side.

But, let me back up and set the stage properly. Like most relationships and overseas positions, everything started off shiny, happy, and new. I moved to Malawi in April 2010 for an incredible two-year research opportunity in an HIV clinic. This would be my fourth two-year position overseas. The public clinic where I would work provided HIV testing, treatment, and care for tens of thousands of patients, and it was known for its high quality services and research. My first six months in Malawi were pretty wonderful—meeting most of the challenges of work and daily living with laughter, finding friends, and getting my cultural bearings. Much like my job, my relationship with Andy started off well. We enjoyed a connection that almost instantly felt right; both my family and my friends loved him. We had spent more than a year together before I left for Malawi, and we both felt secure that our relationship was on solid ground headed for a happy future.

Although Andy had never worked overseas, he was so outgoing, amusing, and generous. I felt certain he would thrive both personally and professionally. I knew it would not be easy, but I imagined that we would rise to the challenges of living in Malawi together, using the strength of our relationship to weather the inevitable ups and downs of life overseas, maximising the benefits of our built-in partnership to take full advantage of adventure and travel that is more difficult to do alone. Five months after I arrived in Malawi, Andy left all that he knew—his job, his home, his friends—to join me. I was elated.

After just a couple months, Andy found a volunteer job he liked, enrolled in an online Master's programme, and made some good friends; we were settled in to our new home. Things seemed to be going well between us. During a romantic Christmas trip to the stunning dunes of Namibia, Andy proposed. Although we told only a few people back home, my engagement ring worn in religiously conservative Malawi legitimised our partnership and gave me additional professional credibility. It spoke of the presumably happy marriage we were bound to have and in which I believed. That new year started well.

By this point, I was well ensconced in my hectic work life. Monitoring and evaluation is anything but glamorous, but the teaching and mentoring components were often energising and affirming even with the stresses of a never-ending, continuously-expanding workload. The work was gratifying: my colleagues worked hard at their jobs and cared deeply about their patients, and the clinics, as a whole, did an excellent job. The work place itself, however, was not without its challenges. First, sharing an office with eight Malawian colleagues meant no head-bashing stress release, no mental-health Skype calls, no secret shopping during work hours, no ten-minute refresher naps. Everything was in the public view, and I was a very obvious public face. Also, although I greatly valued working in a foreign NGO, not having any other expat colleagues was really limiting as far as enjoying work and feeling like there were people with whom to commiserate. I needed a mentor, some other researchers at my level, and outlets for sarcasm and comic relief where my comments were at least sometimes met with smiles rather than blank stares.

In those first six months after Andy's arrival, home brought relief from the stresses of the work place. I could lose my long skirts and non-fitted shirts to roam our sprawling home and yard full of fruit trees in the comfort of shorts and tank tops that would be frowned upon in the conservative country outside our gates. Home meant drinking wine on the porch, playing with the puppies, appreciating the Livingston Turacos (gorgeous, multi-colored birds found only in the region) that drank from our bird bath, and rescuing hedgehogs from the jaws of our dogs during our evening walks around the compound. Home meant cooking comfort food for dinner parties, game nights with our fellow NGO friends, drinking copious amounts of local gin and tonic, and a place to let our guard down completely out of the public eye.

By late February 2011, however, the political situation in Malawi was noticeably deteriorating. The country's previously well-respected president cracked down on the opposition. In response,

Western countries decreased financial support which led to rising prices in stores and at the pumps, compounded by increasing unemployment. As petrol/diesel shortages intensified, water shortages and power cuts followed as the fuel required for the water pumps ran dry and breakdowns in the country's few electric plants remained. All around the country, queues for the petrol stations wrapped through the streets and around blocks, causing traffic nightmares for the few remaining people who had fuel. People slept in their cars in queues, waking up to push their cars a few metres, grateful to receive the precious ten-litre ration of fuel if there was any to be had. We found these first weeks of blackouts and fuel shortages almost exciting, bragging to our friends in the U.S. about surviving the relative hardships of flashlights and little fuel.

For most people in Malawi, the political and fuel crisis had far-reaching repercussions. Although the size and location of my clinic sheltered me from much of what the smaller, lower resourced, or rural clinics endured, national crises hit us like all others. We ran out of key medications and health commodities, including the life-saving, antiretroviral drugs for HIV-infected patients which require strict adherence to the daily pill regimen, leaving some people to spend a few days (or weeks) without their drugs. Patients were audibly angry; the staff were exasperated that their efforts could not change the situation. The drugs, nets, syringes, or gauze were often literally right across the street at the central medical stores, but political stalemates and financial turmoil provided recurrent barriers. While I had felt powerless at work before, it was a whole new level of heartbreak and frustration to watch the Malawian staff experience the same thing.

As I approached my one year mark in April, things at home with Andy, much like in Malawi, began to unravel. The continued hardship of life in Malawi, mostly for others, wore on me. Malawi is one of the poorest countries on the planet, but, with worse than usual droughts, transportation fare increases, price increases, and the government's continued violence towards the opposition, typically-stable Malawi felt on edge. I could not separate myself from the pain of events in the clinic, or tension in the country, even when behind the high cement walls, barbed wire, and the electric fence that surrounded the house. No fuel also meant that my 'escapes hatches' were blocked. Even with my connections at the clinic, and through friends, I couldn't get enough fuel to take a non-essential trip like a weekend getaway to the beach or hiking. With fewer options for respite, my available energy for things outside work waned: I stopped caring what I wore, exercise seemed like a chore, and chocolate was a welcome refuge. I gave much of my energy to my work, leaving less for myself or for Andy. I felt exhausted.

And while I took everything in, Andy seemed to block everything out. I felt like I was watching his heart turn to stone. The juxtaposition of our lives to those outside our gates did not affect him as it affected me. Initially I thought he picked an increasing number of fights because he felt so unsettled leaving everything that he knew, loved, and excelled at by coming to Malawi. But, as time passed, we bickered about more and more little things—like whether 'heighth' was a word, whether we could fire the constantly-complaining gardener, whose turn it was to wash dishes on the weekend when the housekeeper didn't do it. Just a few months after we got engaged, we no longer watched sunsets together on the porch, bird sightings no longer drew us out of the house, candlelight dinners created by roving blackouts held no romance, and the yard swings we had custom made moved only with the wind. No single event, moment, or fight sparked this change; rather, everything became a battle or, worse, a silence that masked a more insidious downward spiral within each of us. We lived in the house together, but I felt completely alone.

With the confluence of a worsening home life and a worsening political climate, I grew less resilient to handle the injustices I encountered at work. One morning, a friend who worked in obstetrics and gynecology told me that she had lost three women the previous day, all due to preventable causes: one died because the assistant nurse didn't want to bother her supervisor; one died because there was no blood available; and one died because the clinician failed to recognise the presence of a second fetus just a week after training on twins. I found out soon after this conversation that the newborn baby of one of the staff nurses had just died of pneumonia. I had met the child, all swaddled, just three days before.

Another clinic story left me equally rattled. An HIV-infected man who started tuberculosis (TB) treatment three days previous died from TB. Although he had also tested HIV positive years ago, he was not yet on treatment. This case was not unusual; however, this situation was different. The deceased man's brother runs an HIV clinic. If even the close family members of Malawi's best trained and most motivated AIDS clinicians could die from accessing treatment too late, what does that mean for others? It was not the clinician's fault in any way but, it put in stark relief the challenge that getting people into treatment, and into treatment on time, was not as simple as increasing knowledge about HIV and TB or improving access to care. Sometimes, or some days, my work and the work of the clinic seemed as futile as spitting on a raging forest fire.

It may sound like I was unprepared for this placement, but I did not go into this naively. I had been overseas for years and worked in international health for almost a decade. I thought this time the worst of the work and overseas life stressors would be diminished by having a supportive partner by my side. With 11 percent of the Malawian population infected with HIV, I knew going in that I would not be laughing all the time. Most days, I actually was just fine: The clinic was full of people doing well on their antiretroviral drugs, people generally appeared healthy, and the sickest patients went to the inpatient center, not to us. Plus, I looked mostly at the clinic data and helped the programmes improve—an indirect link with patient care. But, even a decade after the worst of the AIDS crisis, it still felt like death and dying were too frequent, almost commonplace. Our Social Welfare Committee reported every day on weddings, deaths, births, etc. Some weeks, the ratio was terrible: one wedding to nine funerals. Luckily, in the clinic itself, we experienced few patient deaths. I recall only two deaths during my clinic days, each one followed by what seemed to be an endless, soul-piercing ululation. I cannot imagine what it was like before people accessed treatment. I found it hard to stay tethered to the situation as it was.

Without the benefits of a supportive partner and a refuge at home to buffer the outside world, I found few places to relax or recharge. My ability to build capacity was waning; my ability to find humour in the absurdity of life and work was failing. I felt starved for reassurance, hugs, and support, things which I assumed my partnership would provide, at least in part. By June, work actually became an escape from the morass that had become my home life: weekend duty at the clinic felt like relief rather than burden. Instead of heading home directly after work, I began seeking evening refuge with friends who luckily lived only a few precious drops of fuel away. My feelings of isolation and loneliness were amplified from shouldering the burden of our dissolving partnership in silence, maintaining the façade of happy couple-dom rather than exposing our situation for dissection and scrutiny in the small, and often unforgiving, expat community or to my religious colleagues at work. The relationship was over, but we didn't acknowledge it. It festered. Bedtime at 8pm could often not come soon enough.

Andy's response to the worsening violence, fuel shortages, and silent war between us was to devote himself completely to his online degree coursework and fantasy baseball. I was priority number three, although I often felt lower than that. He sequestered himself in his study on nights and weekends, coming out to eat dinner and to maybe watch a 20-minute TV show from our hard-drive before returning to his hermitage. While he consistently commented that life was easy in Malawi, his actions spoke differently. Before he had been playful and easygoing but now I found him so tightly strung that any small thing—spilled water on shoes, dogs playing

too loudly, a poor play by some basketball player worlds away—
would start him yelling, the veins on his red neck bulging. His
previously funny one-liners were now aimed at me with undertones
of belittlement and condescension. Moving to Malawi seemed to
have humbled him, sparking a reaction of unfounded arrogance. I
think he believed that the move to Malawi was his ultimate gesture
of compromise and prioritisation for me and, therefore, it was up to
me to repay his sacrifice. We did try to talk about our relationship
a few times, but these efforts sputtered and failed. Touching was
also a rarity: both our enormous house and our double-size bed
allowed for a surprising amount of physical distance. I had gained
ten pounds from stress, and I did not find myself attractive. Andy
made clear he noticed my weight gain too.

By late July 2011, things in Malawi worsened further—not
Congo worse—but pretty bad for typically-peaceful Malawi. The
government continued to curtail freedoms for most people while
amassing power and money for themselves. Malawians, usually
quite passive, were fed up. People took to the streets peacefully, but
the government's response came in tear gas and bullets. Looting and
fires followed; people were beaten. Much of it took place, audibly,
down the hill from our house. Things calmed down after a few
weeks, just in time for Andy to leave again for a month in August.
Despite the possibility of continued violence close to home, I felt a
sense of relief at his departure.

Without agreeing to it, both Andy and I used his last month
away in the U.S. to reevaluate and try to find a way to extricate
ourselves from each other and the situation. He used the comfort

of home, the buffer of ten time zones, poor communication links, and his friends to make the break first. But the Skype call, and its aftermath, snapped me out of the malaise that had settled around me like a warm blanket. Isolated and deflated, I had to make a tough admission to myself: I had fallen apart. I had fallen apart slowly, almost invisibly, and in parallel with Malawi. And like Malawi, itself, I had not recognised the depth of my fall.

I don't think that I was clinically depressed. I think that I had become clinically desperate. Desperate to make an impact at work and not feel like my two years were for naught. Desperate to maintain the charade of a happy partnership and evade the shame of my paperless 'divorce'. Desperate to avoid becoming gossip in the small expat community. Desperate to elude the pity or disbelief of my friends or family back in the U.S. who only knew the Andy and the relationship from before we came to Malawi. Desperate not to feel both a professional and personal failure. Desperate to find a safe space for my head and heart before I chewed my nails down to the quick. Desperate to smile and to laugh and to feel relaxed. Desperate for a lifeboat, a way out.

With little additional reflection and reconsideration, I wrote my boss in the U.S. noting that my engagement was off, my partner was leaving, and I needed to leave Malawi four months shy of my contract completion. I did not want to leave my work, but drafting the email felt good. Hitting send gave me an immediate and immeasurable sense of relief.

Although I would leave four months early, I still had to endure those months living with Andy who returned after our phone call, in part, because he had nowhere else to go. In hindsight, I think, "what was wrong with me?" However, at the time, it actually seemed worse to be alone in the house than to be sharing the house with the man I was growing to hate. It seemed worse to face my colleagues and friends with the truth than to continue faking it. Would I do it again? Hell no! In my dreams, I tell him over Skype that he can find his things strewn around the car port when he returned. In my dreams, I un-friend him, I defame him. In my dreams, I tell him to fuck himself for fucking me over and for thinking he was ever good enough for me anyway. In my dreams, I ask him how he could call me fat when he looked like a Perdue chicken: pale fat breasts on tiny legs. I would be free; I would be the heroine. And it would feel good. But feeling good would have to wait. I kept my ring and my game face on.

In those last months, Andy stayed mostly in his study to the relief of both of us. I spent a lot of time crying on the floor of my shower, pushing food around my plate, seeking solace with friends, and finding new homes for my puppies. But, with self-esteem on the horizon, I also leaned into myself and into a few close friends—letting myself finally see and accept reassurance that had likely been there all along. I started wearing things that made me feel a little better, and left those oversized traditional clothing pieces for others. I shaved. I put on some makeup. I jumped rope with abandon. I dropped 20 pounds. I bought some overpriced vegetables and tofu at the fancy expat store. I rekindled a spark of happiness and gained appreciation in those last months: the birds, the elephants, the blooming Jacaranda trees, the hands-on work, the lingering romanticism about expat life, the pleasures that can be experienced best alone or with friends. I pampered myself.

The week I left Malawi in December 2011, my clinic put on a heartfelt goodbye and appreciation party for me—complete with dancing, singing, speeches, tears, crates of Fanta, and a gigantic cake. The comments from my colleagues filled my heart and helped me feel like my professional contributions counter-balanced my personal belly-flop. Being reminded of my accomplishments felt good. In my twenty months in the country, I had helped create treatment protocols to standardise care, published papers to highlight their effective programmes, identified lingering challenges to quality patient care, extended their electronic patient management system for HIV/TB; and wrote grants to help them secure millions of dollars to continue their good work. I felt like part of the team, and I was honoured to have become part of the work family. Hearing their kind words about me and feeling the warmth of their hugs good-bye, I began to forgive myself for cutting my losses and leaving the job early. I began to forgive myself for having fallen for Andy. I began to see more of my own value and lose sight of his. I began.

When I returned to the U.S., I recuperated at my parents' house in the company of family, friends, and my dog—aided by a steady diet of long walks, fresh vegetables, and unconditional love. After taking off the ring, the weight on my hand and on my heart slowly dissolved. The anger and bitterness, initially all consuming, began to subside, replaced by a self-imposed amnesia that erased Andy from my life, before and during our time in Malawi. Now, more than a year out of that placement, I can think about my time in Malawi without a shudder, sometimes even conjuring a smile. I still work in international health for the same NGO, although currently from the headquarters office. Friendships that started in Malawi remain strong, and I am forever grateful. I found a new home on the other side of the U.S. and a new partner with whom to share it. As it turns out, home doesn't have to be hard. Home, in fact, is anything but.

Chad
Introduction

Chad, a landlocked country in central-north Africa, is one of the poorest in the world – and one of the most corrupt, according to Transparency International. It is bordered by Sudan to the east, Libya to the north, Central African Republic to the south, and Niger, Cameroon and Nigeria to the west/southwest. Since its independence from France in 1960, Chad has been wracked by a series of civil wars, political and inter-ethnic conflict and disputes with its neighbours, primarily Sudan and Libya.

In the past decade, conflicts in the Darfur region of Sudan, as well as in Central African Republic (CAR), have resulted in over 400,000 refugees now living in Chad, mostly along the eastern and southern borders. In addition, internal conflicts have created over 90,000 internally displaced persons (IDPs) as of this writing.[1]

Since its founding as an independent state, Chad has frequently been subject to military coups, both successful and attempted. The current president, Idriss Déby, came to power in a coup in 1990, overthrowing the former dictator Hissène Habré – who himself has been charged by the African Union with war crimes committed during his eight-year rule.

During the height of the Darfur conflict, Chad and Sudan fought a proxy war, each accusing the other of arming rebels to fight on their behalf and fomenting political instability on both sides of the border. The creation or expansion of a myriad of rebel groups in

---

1   "UNHCR 2014 Country Operations Profile – Chad". Available from: http://www.unhcr.org/cgi-bin/texis/vtx/page?page=49e45c226.

Chad opposed to Déby's one-party rule led to a series of attempted coups in the mid-2000s, culminating in two ultimately unsuccessful attacks on the capital, N'Djamena, in 2006 and 2008.

One attempted coup began in the eastern town of Abéché in 2006 (the second attempted coup in Chad just that year). A peace agreement signed with Sudan in 2010 largely calmed the situation in the west, although political tensions continue to linger as Déby remains in power.

Though recent oil exploration has raised hopes of potential prosperity, Chad's economy remains at a standstill, and environmental pressures including the desertification of the Sahel and the near disappearance of Lake Chad, continue to contribute to political and ethnic tensions.

Thousands of Chadians who had previously been engaged as mercenaries by Libya's Colonel Muammar Ghaddafi have returned home since his overthrow in 2011, bringing their weapons with them and contribute to ongoing generalized insecurity.

Today, Chad is heavily involved in the current conflict in CAR, with Déby acting as a regional power broker – most recently facilitating the departure from power of the short-lived President of CAR, Michel Djotodia.

Nomads bring their camel to an NGO-sponsored well in Kumahumato, meaning "that which supports cattle" in Somali. The community struggles to keep their cattle alive due to prolonged drought and failed rains in the region near Dadaab, Kenya. ©Jenn Warren

The Coup
Erin Patrick

One of the most predictable things about humanitarian work is how unpredictable it is—especially in terms of security and access to the people we're supposedly there to help. A situation that seems stable and calm can all of a sudden deteriorate; but sometimes when it seems like things can't get any worse, the clouds break. Most of the time, it's hard to tell which is which. And far too often, it becomes a balancing act between trying to address the needs on the ground and managing our own personal security.

In late 2006, I was supposed to be in eastern Chad for six weeks as a consultant to an organisation that assessed cooking fuel options for Darfuri refugees. Three weeks into the mission, I was in Abéché for a break after field visits to the border with Sudan. With eastern Chad destabilised by the conflict in Darfur, anti-government rebels decided to take advantage of the situation to attempt a coup against Chadian president, Idriss Déby. Starting in Abéché, they hoped to move into the capital N'djamena in a 'lightning attack'. Once the fighting started in Abéché, humanitarian staff were forced to hibernate. So began my experience of a coup.

Abéché, 5pm (almost dark), Saturday, 25 November 2006.
The rebels took Abéché this morning. There's nothing quite like waking up to the sound of artillery fire. Actually, I can't say I've ever done that before so I can't really compare it to anything. At first, I didn't even know what it was—I was still sleeping and had earplugs in. I thought maybe it was just drumming, but really bad drumming—which made me think, hmm, maybe that's not really

drumming after all. I dragged myself out of bed to see what the hell was going on, and one of other staff in the guest house where I was staying—I'll call him Wolfgang—grabbed me and told me to pack a 15kg bag right away because we were being evacuated—there was fighting in town and we had to be ready to leave right away. I ran to the bathroom (priorities!) and managed to brush my teeth and put some real clothes on before trying to pack a 15kg bag. Do you know how much is 15kg? I didn't. And, what should count toward the limit? My clothes? Books? My computer? What about my iPod, for heaven's sake!

But it turns out that we didn't have to be evacuated right away—or better put, they couldn't evacuate us because the rebels were everywhere. They'd cut the phone lines but the radios were still working, so we were getting periodic scratchy bits of news. Trucks rumbled down the street with gunmen on top shooting (what I hoped was) into the air. I watched them for awhile, peeking out through the holes in the top of the decorative concrete wall surrounding the little compound, until a bullet whizzed by far too close for comfort and I ran back inside, realising that outdoors was maybe not such a smart place to be after all.

Inside is where we stayed put. For hours. And hours. And hours. It gave me time to rethink my early morning 15kg packing strategy. Definitely take the iPod.

It seemed the rebels were also staying put. They'd taken over the town and dispatched a message that they had no intention of harming the local population, or humanitarian workers. However, all the government, police, and army officials had fled, leaving the town in complete chaos. We heard over the radio that the government army base, the airport, the court, and the jail were all being looted. I kept my fingers crossed that they wouldn't, as Wolfgang helpfully suggested, start on the private houses next. Where would I hide my iPod?

There were five of us in the guesthouse, and a guard, and we couldn't do a damn thing. Luckily, the generator was still working so we just watched bad, old American movies dubbed into French through the day. The head of the organisation sent a message out over the radios that, at least for the moment we would all stay put and hope that the government army forces would decide not to fight for Abéché and would concentrate their efforts instead on protecting N'djamena, where the rebels were supposedly headed. But of course no one really knew where the rebels were headed, or what the government planned to do about it. Do they say that information is the first casualty of war? Oh no, that's truth. Either way we weren't getting much of either.

More importantly, we had no food. There was a giant log of yucca root which we'd found and boiled and eaten for breakfast. No one actually ate in the guesthouses in Abéché because there was a decent café in the office that all the humanitarian staff went to for their meals. So we literally had nothing in the house—and at that point the six of us thought we could be there for days, or weeks... which of course made me start worrying that the Donner Party movie would be next on the TV and someone would get the wrong idea.

But wait! The organisation was prepared for just this sort of problem. There was a padlocked, metal trunk in the kitchen with a note on the top reading: "for emergency use only." We had no idea what was in it but assumed—or at least hoped—that it contained, at minimum, one of the two following items: 1) food; or 2) toilet paper.

But where were the keys? It would make no sense to have an emergency trunk that, in the midst of an emergency, no one can access, right? Well, yes. But that didn't make the keys appear. We turned the house upside down and found no keys, so we took to looking for something to use to just pry the damn thing open. I found a couple of iron drapery rods which, after about 10 minutes of struggle, worked—breaking both the trunk and the rods in the process.

What was inside? FOOD! We wouldn't become the Chadian version of the Donner Party after all! The (now broken) trunk was full of canned ravioli, canned peas, canned fruit, sugar, powdered milk, corn flakes, a carton of cigarettes, playing cards, matches and—TOILET PAPER! Alas, no coffee, but I had already asked the guard to dart over to the teeny, ramshackle shop across the road which the plucky Chadians had re-opened during a lull in the shooting, to buy up all the Nescafe. Bless the nascent capitalism! It was like they'd read our minds.

I thought they could have considered putting some beer in the trunk, though. Can't have everything.

I wondered what was going on outside our gates. The rebels said they didn't mean to hurt the local population but, of course, they did. Some were caught in the crossfire and died, not to mention those in the villages that they took on the way into Abéché. Even while the rebel trucks were coming down our street, though, a fair number of people were out waving at them. I guessed that was a good sign.

I also wondered where the French were—how's that for a common refrain in conflicts in Africa? There was a big French air base right in the middle of town. We hadn't heard a damn thing from them but they must have known whether the Chadian army had fled, or was just regrouping in the surrounding hills to try to retake the town overnight. The morning hadn't exactly been fun, but I had no desire to stay if the army started bombing, nor did anyone else. Wolfgang suggested that it might actually be a good thing that we weren't on the army base—since the Chadian rebels don't like the French any more than the Rwandans do and they might try to take the base next.

All I know is that I have at least another night/day of eating canned peas and playing cards. It could be a lot worse.

Abéché, 6am, Sunday, 26 November 2006.

Last night was not fun. Everyone went to bed early but for some odd reason I found it hard to sleep through the sound of gunfire (not enough practice, I guess?), so I stayed up to see if I could hear anything about the situation on the BBC. No. I took a very, very fast shower, thinking what a ridiculous story it could be:

"Where's Erin, why wasn't she evacuated?"

"Well, we couldn't find her. There was a nice fruity smell coming from the shower, though."

Wolfgang mentioned that he had heard by radio that at least one of the other UN guesthouses was looted at gunpoint last night, either by rebels or military men who had leapt over the security wall, beaten up the guard, and stolen absolutely everything—money, passports, computers, phones, radios, cameras—everything.

"This was just nearby," he tells me. "I hope they don't come for us next."

And, with that, he went back into his room. The only doors that locked in the compound are the plywood doors to our rooms. Even I could break those open in two seconds if I needed to. So, I did the only sensible thing and tried to 'hide' the stuff I thought they might steal. I separated my money and put small amounts everywhere. I stuffed my computer under the mattress (no way they'd look there!). I shoved my passport down my pants and hid the iPod in with my tampons.

There was nothing else to do, and sitting up alone in the dark waiting for armed robbery is just no fun, so I went to bed. There was so much gunfire, though, it was impossible to sleep, and every time a shot seemed close I leapt out of bed waiting to hear the shouts of the people who had surely just shot their way into the compound. What would I do if they did? Should I try to hide under the bed? Run quickly into someone else's room? Who the hell knew? I stayed put until about 5:30am when I finally got up to go pee (priorities), tripped over the stray cat that lives in the compound, fell and sprained my ankle. Perfect timing.

Eventually Wolfgang came in to tell me that more guesthouses were looted overnight along with two UN warehouses. Two things were becoming clear: 1) We were really lucky the night before; and 2) There's no way we'd be so lucky if we stayed a second night.

He got on the radio to say that all of us wanted to move to the French airbase and would walk there if there was no vehicle to take us. How I would do that on a sprained ankle was another question. But, as it turned out, that was pretty much the consensus of the entire rest of the humanitarian community in Abéché. Everyone was radioing that they wanted get out like, NOW, so a plan was being worked up. We were also informed that the government had re-taken the city overnight, which explained all the shooting.

So there I sat, on the couch, foot propped up, eating peanut butter from the jar, drinking my third cup of Nescafé of the morning, glaring at the cat and wondering what 'the plan' would be.

On the plane back to DC, Monday, 27 November 2006
Perhaps I was a bit too harsh on the French earlier.

Two hours after our radio call saying we wanted out, a giant, armed, military convoy was at our door to escort us to the base. The French soldiers apologised for having to frisk us and search our bags, before registering us and giving us a little food and water. *Pas mal.*

That convoy was something else. Having no experience with this sort of thing—and no desire to ever again—I had no idea how it worked. Neither, apparently, did any of the Chadians whose street we lived on. They came out of their houses to watch a bunch of tanks and heavily-armed jeeps surround about 20 white land rovers with a hundred or so aid worker staff inside. No doubt they thought, "Wait! Aren't you supposed to be protection staff? Now that we really need protecting where are you going?"

The little kids stood there on the street waving, as they always do, and for once I didn't know if I should wave back. I mean, what am I saying? "Okay, bye now! I'm the lucky one. I'm from somewhere else so I have these people to protect me. Good luck on your own, little ones!" It was a pretty awful feeling.

At the base, I was told by the organisation that I was to be on the first plane out to N'djamena, but then I was also told by a security officer that N'djamena was likely to be worse than Abéché by nightfall because the rebels were heading there to try to overthrow Déby, so really the safest place to be was the base in Abéché and I should really stay there.

I agreed, she knew better than I did and the base did seem pretty safe, what with all the tanks and fighter jets and soldiers and whatnot. But then, no, I was told by my organisation that I had to fly out. Period. "Ok," I said, wondering how much sense it made to fly people to a more insecure location than the one from which they were coming and couldn't we all be sensible and just go to Cameroon instead? But, no. The plane was scheduled to depart at 4:30—until someone realised we'd land after dark. Not a good idea. So, never mind. The plane wouldn't leave after all. We'd start over in the morning. Bed would be the dirt ground outside. All the mosquito nets had already been taken. Enjoy! The irony was rich. Refugee workers having to live like, well, refugees. Probably a good thing for us all to gain a little more perspective.

I found a corner and sat down to watch the sunset (they really are stunning over the Chadian desert) and try to figure out what the hell had happened over these last couple days. Less than an hour later, the security officer came running over shouting,

"Get on the plane!"

What? To where?

"Either N'Djamena or Yaoundé. Just get on!" I didn't really have a choice (nor a visa for Cameroon, for that matter), but I hobbled to the plane and just as quickly we were in the air.

It's an odd feeling, though, to land and not know where you are. When the plane touched down there was no indication but I recognised it as N'djamena when we got inside the building, since I'd flown through there on my way in to Chad a few weeks before. There was no one there waiting for me, so I called the embassy and was told by embassy staff that I was, in fact, in Yaoundé. I tried to explain that, no, I wasn't, but he just kept insisting that I was most certainly in Cameroon. When I did finally convince him that the airport's name was indeed "NDJAMENA" as written in big bold letters inside the building, sounding more than a little alarmed he told me to run into any UN vehicle available and find the guesthouse—which I did. When I got there, the staff asked "aren't you in Yaoundé?"

Stuck in a town where I shouldn't have been with rebels on the move, I figured I'd better try to get out before they close the airport. I sent a text to my fiancé Erol to see if he could get me on a flight out ASAP. (A bit of advice here—if you ever find yourself stuck in the middle of a coup attempt in an unstable third-world dictatorship and need to get the hell out of there really, really quickly, call Erol. I think he should open a travel agency specialising in humanitarian evacuations).

I have no idea how he did it, but 10 minutes later he wrote back saying, "can you be on a plane at 11:55pm?" Hell, yeah! I limped out of that building as fast as possible and got in the car that was already there to take me to the airport. I did not believe I was actually out until the plane touched down in Paris. But the next day, I was home.

Looking back

It took a few days to find out what had happened to the humanitarian staff still in Abéché. Apparently, they were stuck at the air base for several days, and some were evacuated to Yaoundé for a few weeks. The rebels never did make it all the way to

N'djamena, and fortunately the worst of the fighting in Abéché had already ended by the time of the humanitarian evacuation. But in the chaos, all of the warehouses were looted—the food, the blankets, stoves, everything. As they usually do, though, the operations did eventually get up and running again, and despite a few more coup attempts Chad is now more stable than in 2006. I did go back, a few years later, luckily with a lot less drama the second time around.

When I got back to headquarters after the evacuation my organisation more or less blew off the whole thing and told me that ultimately I was responsible for my own security and there was nothing they could have done. At the time that upset me, but looking back I suppose in many ways, they were right. From then on I've certainly tried to be prepared for anything and to not rely on the hope that the organisation has a good plan in place. Usually, they don't. On more than a few occasions since I've been laughed at by colleagues who wonder why I always travel with peanut butter, Starbucks Via instant coffee and a fully charged little Nokia phone with tons of airtime on it, but—you never know when it will come in handy.

And I still have my humanitarian specialist travel agent, Erol.

Japan – Tōhoku Earthquake and Tsunami
Introduction

An archipelago nation in East Asia, Japan has the third largest economy in the world. With low infant mortality rates, low homicide rates, and high life expectancy Japan performs well in most human development indicators. It is one of the most densely populated countries in the world and the government is democratic.

Japan is subject to a wide range of natural disasters. Situated on the Pacific 'Ring of Fire', Japan has frequent earthquakes, experiences significant typhoons, and is home to a number of active volcanoes.

Given this, Japan has developed extensive structural and procedural disaster mitigation measures. Forty-three percent of Japan's coastline is lined with seawalls or other structures, and evacuation drills are practiced on a national level annually.[1]

Nonetheless, the 9.0 richter scale earthquake that occurred off the coast of Japan on 11 March 2011, and the subsequent tsunami, overwhelmed the country's mitigation abilities. While preparedness certainly saved lives, more than 15,000 people were killed and an additional 2,600 were missing. Nearly 350,000 people were displaced, leading to an immediate effort on the part of both the government, non-profit organisations, and individual volunteers to support their needs in evacuation shelters. These efforts included provision of food, clothing, medical and psycho-social services.

---

1   "Japan". Wikipedia. Available from: http://en.wikipedia.org/wiki/Seawall#Japan.

While the government provided temporary housing, the total destruction of some towns meant that employment had been lost, leading to the need for ongoing, long-term assistance and difficult choices about reconstruction.

Although the non-profit response was carried out mainly by Japanese NGOs (both national and international), a number of international NGOs with existing links to Japan also participated.

Maldivian Woman on the streets of Male, Maldives. ©*Yeva Avakyan*

Accepting Thanks
Malka Older

I didn't expect to be deployed to Japan after the tsunami in 2011 —I didn't think we'd send anyone. Japan has plenty of resources, and a well-educated, high-capacity population. The Japanese have some of the best disaster risk reduction in the world and I'd been using some of their approaches for years in other places as examples of the best practices. What could I offer them? But when the emergency director of the organisation approached me about deploying, he convinced me that, in fact, Japanese speakers with experience in other emergencies could be useful and so I got on a flight to Tokyo.

Japan was different from any other emergency response I'd ever been in. Away from the coast fragmented by the tsunami, the infrastructure and resources of a developed country were still largely functioning. Instead of the UN setting up its specialised humanitarian architecture, the few NGOs which were operational worked almost independently, coordinating with the government as they could.

Tokyo was in a state of shock. Red lights blinked on the omnipresent vending machines indicating that they were out of bottled water, and empty shelves in conveniences stores had hand-written signs apologising for the inconvenience due to extraordinary circumstances. But it was still Tokyo, full of strange fashion and the incongruously hopeful sight of cherry blossoms. The bullet train was not yet running into the disaster area and the state of the roads in the north was uncertain, with an unknown perimeter of radioactivity around Fukushima Daiichi. I flew north, overshooting nearly to Hokkaido, and took the train south to Iwate Prefecture, where we were to be based.

Though it was nearly April, the north was frigid and sometimes snow still fell. The whole region was reeling from the enormity of what had happened. You could see it on the faces of clerks and cashiers, on the signs requesting that guests take the stairs instead of the elevators, to save suddenly precious electricity. Even so, we were not sleeping on the floor of an office or bucket bathing—we stayed in a hotel with internet and light bulbs, and nobody had to share a room. Unlike in Sudan, we did not drive Land Cruisers through deep mud. In Japan, we drove rental cars through the peaceful countryside, listening to the radio, stopping at convenience stores for snacks. Once we got to the coast, though, it was the same as other places: disaster.

The waste that was left by the tsunami on the northeast edge of Japan looked much like the waste I had seen around the southeast of Sri Lanka following the tsunami of 2004—wreckage too crushed and mixed to be identifiable, pieces of wood, tile, and twisted metal. In Japan there were more crushed vending machines and cars; in Sri Lanka there had been more flip-flops. In Sri Lanka, people set up makeshift tent camps outdoors; in Japan they were living in high school gymnasiums, huddled under blankets and curtains trying to stay warm.

In Darfur, when I had amoebic dysentery I went to an NGO clinic and a Sudanese doctor I regularly played volleyball with examined my stool sample under a microscope in front of me. In northern Japan, when I got an eye infection, I went to the eye clinic on the main road of the city where we were living and a Japanese doctor gave me an eye exam.

The clinic in Japan was full of old people who arrived as soon as it opened, fluttering with the excitement at the prospect of a new pair of glasses, or at least something to do for the morning. I was less excited, and had plenty to do, but my right eye had been red and mucky for a week—not ideal for very long working days—so I tried to wait patiently until the doctor could see me. He wanted to look at it through those machines that optometrists use but when he swung it around to look in my eyes it bumped into my cheek.

"Hmm, I guess you have a high nose," he chuckled, employing a rude Japanese stereotype of foreigners. Then, maybe embarrassed about the slur, he asked me whether I was volunteering. I wasn't. I was getting decently paid to provide a service in which I had built up skills and experience throughout my career. But volunteering was the word that was being used in Japanese to describe working in the aftermath of the tsunami. I had a lot to do and not a lot of patience left, so I said, "yes," hoping not to get into a long conversation.

Then, he thanked me. I mumbled something polite and left. The conversation bothered me though. Why should I be thanked? I was getting paid a good salary—more, strangely, than my Japanese counterparts. I was living in a decent hotel. I was doing my job. I didn't see any reason why I should be thanked, especially by someone who saw me as a stereotype. He did not see that it had been my cheek, not my nose, that he had bumped with the machine, because he expected foreigners to have protruding noses. He had no idea who I was or what I was doing but because of a stereotype he had about volunteers I was to be thanked.

Back at our hotel, I was putting off getting ready for bed and fiddling with my blog when the room started rattling. Then it ratcheted up to pounding, hammering, and shaking.

There had been plenty of aftershocks in the two weeks since I arrived in Japan, long resonating vibrations or gentle bumps that I felt through my mattress while in bed. I had even smiled during the first aftershock, because I felt so much safer in a Japanese building than I had felt in an Indonesian one during the aftershocks which followed the 2009 earthquake in Padang. But this was different. I ran out of the room and into the lurching hallway. It was like turbulence in an airplane, with no seatbelts; it was a roller-coaster with no tracks. The lights dimmed suddenly, changing the ambience from garish to ghostly as the power cut and the emergency electricity automatically switched on. I ran to the emergency exit and tried the door but the lock wouldn't give. The whole building was shaking, the potted plants by the elevator had already toppled over, and pictures were falling off the walls. It can't hold out, I thought. I couldn't stand up any longer, and huddled on the floor. The building is going to go down, and here I am stuck because this damn emergency door isn't working!

Then, the shaking slowed and lessened to the point where the pounding of my heart was louder than the rattling of the building. My Japanese colleagues came out of their rooms. They had been sheltering under their desks, which is what they were trained to do during a tremor. That response made more sense to me when I returned to my room. It looked like the Rolling Stones had been partying in there. A heavy mirror had fallen off the wall; the water glass was broken in shards. Under the desk would have been the safest place to be. I grabbed my bag and went back out into the hall. One colleague easily flipped open the lock on the emergency door, and we made our way, shakily, down the five flights of outdoor emergency stairs.

Nobody wanted to stay on the fifth floor of that hotel any longer. One of our Japanese colleagues had rented an apartment and ten of us crowded onto a few futons on her floor, covered with blankets and coats. The electricity stayed out that night, and the ground kept rumbling with threatening aftershocks, keeping us on edge with the fear that maybe the next one would be even bigger than the last.

Tired from a sleepless night, the next morning I joined my colleagues getting in the car for a field visit. I remembered that you need electricity to pump gas out of the ground. If the power didn't come back on soon, gasoline would start to run out. I wondered if we should use the gas we had in our tanks to head to a working airport and get out of there instead of going on another assessment visit. I looked at the closed 24-hour stores, which had put hasty signs announcing they were temporarily shut, and I wondered how long food would hold out. And safe water. During that night and the next day, I thought about the doctor who thanked me. I still did not need, or deserve, it. I did not want to be thanked. I wanted to go home.

But, of course, I didn't go home. We went on our assessment visit to the island of Oshima, where the people told us that their electricity, out since the disaster, had only just been reconnected the day before, and was now cut again. We poked our heads into the evacuation center, a quiet gymnasium that had been subdivided into family-sized plots with cardboard boxes and draped futons. They had been there for almost a month now and they had no idea when they were going to be able to move anywhere else. The residents had lost everything but, even so, they had organised. Most spent their days running the same soup kitchens from which they ate or picking quietly through piles of donated clothes for something that might fit. People were polite to us. Nobody asked why we weren't hurrying up and getting them better food or more blankets.

Surveying that small community, it was hard not to feel ashamed. After all, I had signed on for this. I went there knowing, more or less, what I was getting into. I had a home to go back to. The next day, when most of the power would be restored, I would have a hot shower. For the majority of the displaced it would be another month or two until they had access to such a luxury.

When I think about the disaster in Japan now, I remember how easy it is to get unmoored when everything starts shaking beneath your feet. The impulse is to grab what you need for yourself and your family, then grab a bit more than you need, in case it takes longer for things to normalise, then a bit more. I am again and again impressed with those people who endured that shaking with quiet patience in the convention centers, schools and public gyms, who distributed aid as fairly as they could. I think about the kind of trust it takes not to panic, the faith they had to do things together, in groups or communities, instead of alone, the belief they had that things would go better if they thought about more than themselves. It is something that I've seen again and again in the aftermath of many different disasters: the winding, long lines for petrol in West Sumatra, waiting quietly and without argument; community leaders in Darfur insisting that they get enough goods for their whole group, not just a part of it. Parachuting into an emergency, it is easy to forget how difficult that is, until something happens to shake our faith in our own safety nets.

But when I think of that unpleasant eye doctor, I remember another lesson from Japan too. I hate being perceived as a martyr, or a hero. I spend a lot of time trying to convince people that my work is not a sacrifice, that it's different from volunteering, that it's a job I enjoy and which is usually very safe. But sometimes, in my zeal not to be taken for something I'm not, I forget that there are parts of the job that are scary, difficult, and occasionally dangerous, and I do those parts of the job too. Hopefully what I did was helpful; for all the monitoring and evaluation that we did, I will still never know how to measure my contribution. But I am fairly sure that, as usual, I got more out of it than I gave.

Which is to say I still don't like to be thanked. But I'm working on it.

Girls participating in a youth group in Motot, South Sudan ©Kelsey Hoppe

Author, Photographer & Editor Biographies

Mia Ali (Author & Editor): Mia has held a variety of humanitarian and development roles for INGOs and private sector organisations in East and West Africa, the Pacific and the UK. An evening class ignited a passion for writing and she is currently working on her first novel, based on her experiences overseas. With her husband, she has recently launched a social enterprise (www.aidworks.org.uk), which helps organizations in Africa to strengthen their systems and supports local and international development workers to reach their potential. She lives in Sheffield, UK.

Yeva Avakyan (Photographer): Born and raised in the former Soviet Republic of Armenia, Yeva is also a citizen of the world and a keen observer of people and places. At 13, she picked up her first camera and by 15 was barring her family from the only bathroom in the house to develop pictures. At 18, she was living in the USA studying Spanish and sociology, and launching her international career. She went on to study public policy, public administration, organizational development, and evaluation, and to work and photograph in countries around the globe. She currently works for World Vision in Washington, D.C., as Senior Gender and Evaluation Advisor, where she is privileged to help communities around the world address gender-based violence. She is passionate about discovering new foods, the colours and textures of bricks and old buildings, getting lost in unfamiliar places, piano, jazz, family, yoga, and, of course, good cappuccino!

Wendy Bruere (Author): At last count, Wendy has lived in seven different countries in the Middle East, West Africa, and Asia. She's worked for UN agencies, NGOs and media outlets. Her career 'path' is more a career web, and has taken her to Nigerian slums, refugee camps in Jordan and Iraq, natural disaster hit areas in Indonesia, and remote Timorese villages. It's also seen her trying to explain herself to police officers in several distant corners of the globe. In between chasing adventures and hoping that somehow some of what she does may help make the world a better place, she lives in Melbourne. She tries to maintain hobbies, like rock-climbing, and, despite all available evidence to the contrary, still thinks challenging men to push-up competitions is a reasonable pick up technique.

Miranda Bryant (Author): Miranda recommends a mid-life career switch to one and all. After working as a small-town newspaper reporter and editor for 12 years in Minnesota and Washington states (USA), she decided to join the Peace Corps. Having never travelled abroad, she found herself living for two years in Kazakhstan as a public health volunteer. To her surprise, she went on to obtain a master's degree in international public health and changed professions. She has since worked in South Sudan, Malawi, Papua New Guinea and Pakistan, focusing on malaria prevention and treatment, safe water initiatives, and family planning in order to reduce death and illness among women and their children. Miranda is honoured that her essay was chosen for this body of work and is thrilled to share the pages with some of her dearest friends.

Caryl Feldacker (Author & Photographer): Caryl is a committed idealist whose sarcasm and goofiness allows her to remain mostly sane while working in sub-Saharan Africa. Her passion for travel and for trying to make the world a better place led her to work in international health, starting in the field of population/environment linkages and moving through rural health into her current work in HIV prevention, treatment, and care. After finishing her MPH at Tulane, she spent two years in the

Peace Corps in Ecuador, only to return to the United States long enough to land a 2-year placement in rural Brazil, first in the Amazon and then in the Pantanal. Wanting a break from overseas life, Caryl brought her Amazon mutt dog, Red Dog, back from Brazil and completed her Doctorate at UNC/Chapel Hill in 2009. After surviving the four years of her PhD, Caryl spent two years in Malawi working in an HIV clinic as an evaluation technical advisor. Currently, Caryl is a Clinical Assistant Professor and Research and Evaluation Advisor in the Department of Global Health at the University of Washington. She travels frequently to Mozambique and Zimbabwe for work, but she is always eager to return home to her partner, son, and Red Dog in Seattle, Washington.

Olivia French (Editor): Olivia French received her degree in English Literature and Language from the University of British Columbia and is currently pursuing her Juris Doctor at the University of British Columbia Faculty of Law in Vancouver, Canada. She has lived across Canada, as well as in England, New Zealand, and Nepal. She has a life-long passion of involvement in humanitarian work and environmental causes. She works as a yoga instructor and editor in Vancouver, BC.

Miranda Gaanderse (Author): Miranda inherited a love for the great outdoors from her father, and itchy feet for travel from her mother. While countless childhood hours spent exploring maps in atlases, encyclopaedias and magazines did not translate into a reliable sense of navigation, it did spur a fascination with the world outside her hometown of Kanata, Canada. Miranda studied politics and international affairs, and joined the humanitarian relief, recovery and development field in 2005. She has since worked for donors, NGOs and UN agencies with a focus on refugee protection, human rights of internally displaced persons

(IDPs), post-conflict governance, and security sector reform. Her studies and work have taken her to Rwanda, South Sudan, Sweden, Switzerland, Tanzania, and Uganda. She is presently based in Juba, South Sudan, where she supports protection programming for IDPs in various parts of the country. When she is not in meetings, writing reports, riding in helicopters or camping in field sites, she enjoys making travel plans with her husband – an adventurous astrophysicist who shares her passion for exploration.

Emilie Greenhalgh (Author & Photographer): Emilie grew up listening to her father's stories about climbing mountains in the Andes and traveling across the African continent in a VW Van, sparking her interest in travel at an early age. Following an eye-opening study abroad experience in Senegal in college she decided to join the Peace Corps, spending two years working on small enterprise development and NGO capacity building in Cameroon. After attending graduate school for African studies and international economics, Emilie also worked in Morocco, Eastern DRC, and Afghanistan. She is truly passionate about agroenterprise, small enterprise development, and gender issues. Emilie recently moved to Washington, DC to explore life in the world of donors and policymakers, where she will focus on innovative programming to reduce poverty for women in Africa. In addition to her love of travel and development issues, Emilie also considers herself to be a bit of a foodie and wine lover, and hopes to participate in a yoga teacher training someday soon.

Kirsten Hagon (Author & Editor): Kirsten started off her human rights and humanitarian career in Australia, where she worked as a lawyer and advocate for asylum seeker rights. Unfortunately that work was clearly unsuccessful as not much has changed since, and it's an issue she remains passionate and frustrated about. She has since then moved between UN Agencies and NGOs, even an international court, as well as between various countries and regions – Sudan (Darfur), Egypt, OPT, Uganda, Chad, Cote D'Ivoire, DRC. New York, Vancouver and Melbourne also crop up on this list. Over this time she has learnt to rock-climb and backcountry ski, and in all of these places she tried to dance - to anything and as often as possible. Until recently she headed up Oxfam's UN Liaison office in New York, engaging UNSC members and UN Agencies on humanitarian and protection issues. She is currently based in Jerusalem with her husband who she met in Darfur (their first date was wading in a full wadi) where she has been researching the impacts of donor counter-terrorism measures on aid and is contemplating the more terrifying prospect of starting a family.

Ali Hayes (Author): Ali has worked for many years on humanitarian responses, peacekeeping and the protection of civilians. She has worked with a range of non-governmental organizations, the United Nations and the UK Government in conflict and disaster-affected areas, including Darfur, Bosnia, Pakistan, Haiti and Mali. Originally qualifying as a lawyer, Ali has a Masters in 'Global Governance and International Security' with a specialization in Human Rights and International Humanitarian Law. Ali moved to New York to help establish the Protection of Civilians Unit at the UN Department of Peacekeeping and currently works for the UN's Special Representative on Preventing Sexual Violence in Conflict. Her real bosses are her two little girls, who remind her that the most important place to be is with them.

Kelsey Hoppe (Author, Photographer & Editor): Kelsey currently works for the Pakistan Humanitarian Forum (PHF), an organisation of international

NGOs providing humanitarian assistance in Pakistan. Previously, she worked in a range of different humanitarian and development roles in a variety of countries, including Sudan, South Sudan, Uganda, Indonesia, and Ukraine. She was born in California, attended university at George Washington University in Washington, DC, and is currently completing a Masters at Cambridge University, UK. She lives in Islamabad, Pakistan.

Rachael Hubbard (Author): I grew up in a quiet mountain town in Appalachia where my parents chose alternative education and home schooled my siblings and I. Home schooling, and my parents' encouragement was the foundation I needed to support my ideas and feed my adventurous spirit. My midwifery journey started while I was studying Painting at Hungry Creek Art School in New Zealand. I became friends with an amazing English midwife and my French teacher as well had her babies at home. I grew up familiar with and respecting midwifery, but did not develop a personal interest until meeting these wonderful ladies. In 2010, I moved back to West Virginia and attended Sacred Mountain Midwifery School on Spruce Knob, West Virginia. I had an incredible experience at school with my teachers and classmates as I learned the secrets of midwifery. I had immediate clarity about becoming a midwife, and zealously perused my apprenticeship. I apprenticed with Ruth Ann Colby Martin in West Virginia, and then spent one year internationally between the Philippines, Trinidad and Tobago and Uganda as a midwife student. My heart for midwifery is to serve women both in my local community, and to continue to work in the developing world. I currently work as a home birth midwife in Virginia and West Virginia.

Lucy O'Donoghue (Author): Lucy has been engaged in aid and development work since 2008 in Vanuatu, Thailand, Democratic Republic of Congo,

South Sudan and Pakistan. To balance out, her academic background in oft perceived 'wafty' (but wonderful) subjects like sociology, economics, theology and philosophy, Lucy is currently completing an MSc in Public Health through the University of London/London School of Hygiene and Tropical Medicine. Lucy and her husband JP hail from opposite ends of the earth, New Zealand and Ireland respectively. Along with Billy, their Khyber Shepherd, they have wound up in Bangkok for the time being, still a bit shell shocked by life in an urban jungle.

Tracy O'Heir (Author): Tracy grew up in Chicago and, while she loves her hometown, has been on a search for nicer winters since she was 18. Currently she is a Disaster Operations Specialist with the Office of US Foreign Disaster Assistance (OFDA) at the US Agency for International Development, the US Government office which responds to foreign humanitarian emergencies. During Tracy's 'first career' in social work, she worked with people living with HIV and immigrants and refugees in the United States. She started her career as a humanitarian worker with the Jesuit Refugee Service in South Sudan from 2002-2004, and later worked in South Sudan for Catholic Relief Services from 2006-2009. From 2009 to 2011, she served as the Senior Program Manager for Disaster Response for InterAction, the largest alliance of US-based international NGOs. Tracy has also worked on responses to humanitarian crises in Syria, Zimbabwe, and Uganda. She graduated from Fordham University with a MA in International Political Economy and Development in 2006. She speaks Arabic and also studied in Egypt at the American University in Cairo in 2005.

Ros Nicholson (Editor): Ros has worked for a number of NGOS in humanitarian responses and development programmes since 1998.

Starting out in South Sudan she has also lived in Eritrea, Ethiopia, Sierra Leone, and Sri Lanka where she developed addictions to fine coffee and year round sunshine. A nurse with a Masters in Public Health in Developing Countries, she now works as a freelance consultant primarily working on health based research and writing projects. Originally from Cornwall in the UK Ros is in the midst of building a house in Australia and considers both countries 'home'. Currently enduring a British winter Ros hopes to join her husband in Damascus in the near future.

Malka Older (Author): Malka is an aid worker, a writer, and a PhD candidate exploring the dynamics of multi-level governance and disaster response. Her work experience includes supporting global programs and agency-wide strategy as a disaster risk reduction technical specialist; designing and implementing economic development initiatives in post-disaster context; and supervising a large and diverse portfolio as Director of Programs in Indonesia. She has responded to emergencies in Sri Lanka, Uganda, Darfur, Indonesia, Japan, and Mali, in the last three as Team Leader.

Erin Patrick (Author): Erin has been working in refugee policy and humanitarian response programs since 2001, focusing mostly on protection and issues affecting women, including several years spent leading the global Safe Access to Firewood and alternative Energy (SAFE) initiative. She is currently working with UNICEF on gender-based violence in emergencies and has also worked for the Women's Refugee Commission, Migration Policy Institute, Human Rights Watch and for terrorism analyst and author Peter Bergen, among others. Most of Erin's work in the field is in east and central Africa. Sometimes (usually in the midst of a 50 hour flight) she questions her sanity, but it's also hard to imagine doing anything else. She lives in New York with her husband/personal security coordinator, and together their second full-time job is restoring their 125-year brownstone, mostly with dental tools. Erin has a Master's from Johns Hopkins University School of Advanced International Studies (SAIS) and an honorary PhD in wood stripping.

Melissa Phillips (Author): Melissa has worked for many years with refugees and asylum-seekers in Australia, the UK, South Sudan and North Africa with NGOs and the UN. She likes to think her work contributes to improved conditions for displaced persons however if you ask Melissa's 4-year old niece what she does, she'll tell you she is always on 'holidays'. Melissa is an avid reader of tales from the field, from biography to fiction, and jumped at the opportunity to contribute to this anthology. A passionate feminist, Melissa also believes in the unique perspective that women bring to aid and development work. In her spare time in the field Melissa has learnt Congolese dancing, Arabic and contributed to the first edition of the Bradt Guide to Sudan (by Paul Clammer, published in 2010, later revised 2013). She is an Honorary Fellow at the University of Melbourne and shares a birthday with everyone's favourite humanitarian – Angelina Jolie.

Ansar Rasheed (Photographer): Ansar has worked for over 14 years in humanitarian aid. For over five years (2005-2010) she worked on community-based interventions on HIV/AIDS raising awareness, working closely with adolescents, MSM, and sex workers from the most vulnerable areas in Aden. Ansar believes that to enable service provision to children, children themselves should be empowered and that their voices should be heard and highly considered.

Rebekah Rice (Photographer): Rebekah (Becks) never really knew what to do with her life until the final year of her undergraduate degree when decided to do something about the millions of people in the world without access to clean water. After further study, she began a career in the UK water industry, with the plan of working overseas one day. In November 2006, she got the opportunity flying to South Sudan for her for her first assignment implementing water and sanitation projects. Despite being naive and unprepared latrines were still built, boreholes drilled and household sandfilters installed! From there she worked in Emergency Response and became known as 'bush gal'. After four years in South Sudan, Becks is back in England. She is still in the water industry and happy to be called a water geek (turn that tap off when cleaning your teeth!). Back in England, she loves to do anything outdoorsy - mountain-biking, climbing, running, camping and co-runs the youth group at her local church as well as being Vice Secretary for the Chartered Institute of Water and Environmental Secretary (CIWEM). Becks still has a huge desire to work overseas again and is determined to go out again... somewhere...one day...

Steph Roberson (Author): Steph developed a fascination with travel and other cultures at a young age, growing up in Hong Kong before her family relocated to the UK. After graduating with a degree in English Literature and Classical Studies, she worked as a teacher in South Korea and Kuwait before moving into the humanitarian sector and completing an MSc in Humanitarian Programme Management. Steph has worked in Nepal, India, South Sudan and the Philippines, specialising in project management, capacity building and emergency food security & livelihoods, and getting onto first-name terms with various parasites along the way. She is currently working at an INGO in Oxford, developing capacity building materials and supporting emergency responses worldwide.

Steph firmly believes that little things in this world can make a big difference. She loves travelling, Thai food, cats, knitting and making patchwork quilts, and maintains a healthy belief that the machines are out to get her. When it comes to urban legends about people being injured by anything technological, rest assured that at least two of those legends began with Steph.

Roberta Romano (Author): Born in southern Italy, Roberta always felt she was bound to work in, and for, the developing world. She has lived most of her life chasing the dream that changing our world is possible and that peace, justice and human dignity are not utopias but realities to be defended. She hopes to spend the rest of her life making this dream true. She studied Political Science, International Law and Human Rights and has worked as a Protection Officer and manager of development projects in emergencies and post-conflict scenarios. Roberta has lived and worked for different international organizations in Zimbabwe, Albania, Sudan and Uganda. She loves when new and different people meet and welcome each other as members of the same kind, creatures of the same God. She currently lives and works in Gulu, Northern Uganda, with her wonderful husband and children.

Helen Seeger (Author):   Born in India to missionary parents, Helen spent her childhood in Pakistan and Thailand. Completely jaded by overexposure to stunning mountains and crystal clear seas, she remembers brief periods back in the UK as miserable, wet, grey and confusing. Returning to the UK and France to study law, Helen discovered the joys of pubs, festivals, punting and the British public transport system. Failing to convince herself or anyone else that commercial law was her fate, she hightailed it back to warm and colourful Pakistan, working first on a maternal, newborn and child health project in the earthquake-affected area, and then supporting shelter, health and communications responses to the massive floods of 2010. Moving on to Yemen, Helen supported a range of protection and migration projects. She has recently returned to the UK to complete a masters' degree and spend some more time in pubs, in parks and on buses.

Jess Shaver (Photographer): Jess is an Educationalist that likes to take photographs but isn't very technical or at all professional about it. Sometimes she's lucky (and feels honoured to have a picture selected for this book). Jess has worked as a teacher, a teacher trainer; has managed and coordinated Education projects and provides technical advice and support in various countries, including The Gambia, Sudan, South Sudan, Ethiopia and Somalia. Oh, and the UK. Jess currently lives in Nairobi with her husband, two 'shenzi' (Kenyan mutt) dogs, four chickens and varying numbers of rabbits (they eat them). She speaks Arabic like a 2-year old child, a skill that is rapidly deteriorating as she jumps around between the beautiful and varied sounds of Kiswahili, Somali, Amharic, Dinka and 'Juba' Arabic languages.

Carmen Sheehan (Author, Photographer & Editor): Born in the United States and raised abroad, Carmen developed the "travel bug" around the age of four. Upon graduating high school, she made a brief return to the USA to complete her Bachelors in Biology. Determined to make her first million by the age of 21, Carmen then joined the Peace Corps, where she served as a Health Volunteer in the beautiful mountains of Ecuador. Needless to say, she didn't come anywhere close to making that first million, but the pursuit of world peace and friendship is sure to become lucrative any day now.

Sticking with this theory, Carmen went on to complete her MPH/ MSW at Tulane, followed by a number of years working on emergency aid projects based in Darfur, northern Uganda, and Mozambique. She eventually returned to the USA for a spell, adjusting gradually to the consistent electricity and uncanny variety of cheeses, and transitioning her focus from emergency to development work. When not otherwise engaged in World Peace, Carmen enjoys spending time with her husband and daughter, catching up with friends, drinking coffee, going for long runs, and – ever the master of moderation – drinking more coffee.

Ruth Townley (Author): Ruth was born in England and lives in Sydney. She was the impressionable age of four when Band Aid UK commenced its campaign. She remembers seeing the television images and deciding that when she grew up, she'd travel in Africa. She also spent a lot of time hanging around a Salesian Boys Town. It was much later that she realised the big boys she followed about were quite troubled young men. They were just kind to her. Small wonder, really, that Ruth's life has involved a lot of volunteering: including with refugees in Sydney, as an assistant midwife in rural Philippines (she was started on reception but got promoted for not speaking the language), and with street kids in Tanzania. Unmanageable rage at Australia's treatment of asylum seekers contributed to a two-year stint in northern Uganda. Ruth's career has included coordinating an NGO for disadvantaged children. She is a psychologist, currently working in a hospital with chronically suicidal patients. Outside work, she is fond of curry festivals and costume parties, and is smug about owning an ancient convertible, given her sister's admonishment when Ruth was 19 that if she didn't get a real job, she'd never have a sports car.

Jenn Warren (Photographer & Editor): specialises in communications and photography for the humanitarian and development sectors. Jenn has worked for a wide range of government, donor, UN and NGO clients including USAID, UKaid, Médecins Sans Frontières, International Committee for the Red Cross, Amnesty International, Save the Children, PSI, the National Democratic Institute, Sonke Gender Justice Network, UNHCR, UNICEF and UNESCO. Her photography and writing has been published in the Sunday Times Magazine, TIME, Rolling Stone, BBC News Online and Al Jazeera English, among others. Jenn teaches photography, and is proficient in Arabic and American Sign Language. Her photography is exhibited and collected internationally.

Kati Woronka (Author): As a student, Kati secretly dreamed of backpacking around the Middle East. So when she had the opportunity to study Arabic in Syria, she went – and quickly fell in love with life in Syria. After conquering Arabic, or attempting to do so, she became an academic researcher and fulfilled her dream, travelling around the region to interview disenfranchised women, religious minorities and refugees. Her research led to a passion for education, community reconciliation, and civil society: the kind of stuff international NGOs are meant to care about. Kati started working with Iraqi refugees in Syria in 2007, and her role there as a volunteer coordinator marked the beginning of a fascinating journey chasing misery in places such as Kosovo, Darfur, Haiti, East Timor, and most recently back in the Middle East responding to the crisis in Syria. She now lectures in International Development at the University of East London. Kati recently published a novel based on her research about Syrian culture, entitled *Dreams in the Medina.*